Panache

Montreal's *flair* for kosher cooking

edited by Shawna Goodman-Sone

THE AUXILIARY OF THE SIR MORTIMER B. DAVIS JEWISH GENERAL HOSPITAL

Panache

Library and Archives Canada Cataloguing in Publication

    Panache : Montreal's flair for kosher cooking.

Includes index.
ISBN 0-9737346-0-4

    1. Cookery, Jewish. 2. Kosher food. I. Sir Mortimer B. Davis
Jewish General Hospital. Auxiliary.

TX724.P35 2005   641.5'676   C2005-900620-X

First printing March 2005
Second printing October 2005
Third printing February 2009

Published by The Auxiliary of the Sir Mortimer B. Davis Jewish General Hospital
    3755 chemin de la Côte Ste. Catherine, #A 018
    Montréal, Québec H3T 1E2
    E-mail: lkaplans@aux.jgh.mcgill.ca | Website: www.jgh.ca

Cover painting: Y. Chaki, Still Life with Flowers 0437, 50 x 50 inches, oil on canvas, 2004
Cover food photography: Nicholas Amberg
Food styling: Lucie Richard

Printed in Canada.
All product / brand names are trademarks or registered trademarks of their respective trademark holders.

Callawind
Custom Cookbooks

Produced by Callawind Custom Cookbooks
A division of Callawind Publications Inc.
3551 St. Charles Boulevard, Suite 179, Kirkland, Quebec H9H 3C4
E-mail: info@callawind.com   Website: www.callawind.com
Copy editing: Lesley Cameron | Design: Marcy Claman | Indexing: Jane Broderick

contents

note from the Auxiliary

The most valuable asset a hospital can have is the support of the people it serves. The Sir Mortimer B. Davis Jewish General Hospital was originally established as a result of community solidarity, and today it continues to be a living testament to the goodwill, perseverance and dedication of its doctors and staff, and to the thousands of volunteers who perform miracles—large and small—every day.

In 1936, a group of involved women founded the Women's Auxiliary. Designed to stimulate and coordinate volunteer service and to increase the usefulness and efficiency of the Hospital, the Auxiliary was also charged with increasing public understanding and support for the Hospital itself. Today the Auxiliary numbers over 4,000 members, includes both men and women, and is active in an astonishing variety of fundraising initiatives.

The product of one of these initiatives—*Panache,* our gourmet kosher cookbook—was created, developed and brought to completion through the dedication and determination of Shawna Goodman-Sone. Shawna, a chef and caterer, lent her cooking skills, her drive, her editing prowess and her inspiration to this labour of love. Shawna's inspiration was the catalyst that brought together cookbook committee chair Leslie Spector-Cons and an enthusiastic group of testers and tasters who evaluated each recipe, produced every one in their homes and ensured that the quality of the product was as strong as the ingenuity of its premise. Credit and thanks must be given as well to food stylist Lucie Richard, photographer Nicholas Amberg, cookbook designer Marcy Claman and internationally renowned artist Yehuda Chaki, who created the original oil painting featured on the cover of *Panache.*

Panache reflects Montreal's rich and diverse ethnic communities: Ashkenazi and Sephardic recipes abound, as do modern variations on French and Italian classics. All the recipes are kosher, and include possible variations, chef's tips and other general information that even the most seasoned chef will find useful.

Our Hospital, like many, is continuously faced with the challenge of providing rapid and efficient service to its patients and community at the same time as cutbacks in government funding and a continuing need for the purchase of state-of-the-art technology. The Auxiliary, with projects such as this one, helps the Hospital meet these challenges head-on. Specifically, the revenue generated from the sales of *Panache* will enable the Auxiliary to purchase much-needed equipment for the Emergency Department. In this way, the Auxiliary can continue to fulfill the goals and aspirations set out by its founders 70 years ago.

Ultimately, the patients of the Sir Mortimer B. Davis Jewish General Hospital are the beneficiaries of your purchase of *Panache.* On their behalf, as well as on behalf of the Auxiliary, we thank you.

Hela Boro and Eileen Fleischer
Co-Presidents

note from the cookbook editor

Jewish dietary laws (Kashruth) teach us that the privilege of eating should be regarded with the utmost awareness and respect. In addition, Judaism has a high regard for the role that food plays in enriching people's lives. It was this idea—ideal, really—that was the genesis of Panache.

Putting together *Panache* has been an incredible and delectable journey into the heart and soul of Montreal—a multicultural city bursting with sophisticated cuisine. When I started this project, I was genuinely excited by the opportunity to sample both the heirloom and modern recipes kept close to the hearts of some of Montreal's most accomplished professional and private chefs and cooks.

The *Panache* team started by gathering over 400 recipes with the goal of finding Montreal's most novel and appetizing culinary treasures. What fun! Over cold winter months and hot summer days, a group of 100 volunteers tested and evaluated scores of recipes based on a rigorous set of criteria (appearance, flavour, accessibility of kosher ingredients, cooking time and novelty). *Panache* reflects the culmination of these efforts and represents the best of Montreal's joie de vivre, gastronomic sophistication and ethnic diversity.

Panache could not have happened without the creativity and dedication of the special group of dedicated community volunteers who came together to work on this project. I would like to thank everyone who contributed their time, effort and financial resources to bring *Panache* to life. I am particularly grateful to the Auxiliary presidents for their energy and encouragement over the past 18 months. I would also like to thank my family for supporting me and sampling all the culinary creations that were sent their way.

To me, *Panache* represents a gift for ourselves and our children—a legacy of the best cooking in Montreal. I hope you experience as much joy in your kitchen as I have in mine. Bon appétit!

Shawna Goodman-Sone

Shawna is a culinary training graduate of the Natural Gourmet Cooking School and a pastry arts graduate of the Institute of Culinary Education (formerly Peter Kump's Cooking School), both in New York City. She has also trained at the Cordon Bleu school in Paris. For the past 11 years, Shawna has been teaching, catering and cooking for clients in Montreal (where she lives), New York, Philadelphia and Toronto.

note from the cookbook committee coordinators

Experiences and memories are what keep us going. For many of us here, an experience we'll remember with true fondness is the terrific feeling of pulling together to make Panache *such a success.*

No sooner had we begun than we discovered how much effort was needed to participate in a major volunteer project while continuing to juggle our busy schedules. But just as quickly, we learned something else: people become very devoted when they sign on to a project of this kind, especially when they're aware of the crucial role it can play in generating revenue for an important cause.

Working on *Panache* was a wonderful learning experience, involving an incredible group of fundraisers, collectors, testers, tasters, marketers and editors. As each committee organized a strong team of its own, we all gained a renewed appreciation for the commitment of our volunteers in completing their tasks.

We hope *Panache* will bring special meaning to cooks with a taste for Jewish cuisine. Even more appetizing is the support that the Auxiliary will be able to provide to the Jewish General Hospital's Emergency Department through the proceeds of the ongoing sale of this cookbook.

As an added bonus, all of the recipes and ingredients in *Panache* are strictly kosher. Thus, anyone can use our cookbook, with no substitution of ingredients. And this brings up yet another highlight: the connection to our roots. It's heartening to know that tradition is still such a vital element of the Jewish home. We're proud of the part we can play in maintaining those traditions while adding a tasty new twist of our own for the current generation and, we hope, for many more to come.

Leslie Spector-Cons—Chair
Allison Boman, Dana Caplan, Yael Elfassy, Robyn Krane, Stephanie Raby-Naimer

note from a friend

The Jewish General Hospital opened its doors on October 4, 1934, and it soon became apparent that a Women's Auxiliary could be of inestimable aid to the hospital.

So in 1936, wise women laid strong foundations for service and dedication, which have been the keynote down through the years. We have ever been mindful of the high ideals and principles upon which our Auxiliary was founded, prospering and growing both in strength and in stature.

Today, women and men of many age groups and cross-sections of the community contribute their personal effort in the same spirit of selflessness and cooperation that has epitomized every phase of auxiliary endeavour. Their enthusiasm and zeal on behalf of Auxiliary works bespeaks their deep concern for the health and welfare of others. Wherever and whenever needed, whether for service, educational help or financial help, our Auxiliary has always been conscious of its close bond with the hospital.

Throughout the years, our activities have continued to reflect the true meaning of our existence and have fulfilled the high hopes and aspirations of our founders. The past has been glorious and fruitful. Let us continue to strive so that our future may continue to be strong and meaningful and we may truly say, "We come in no spirit of vainglory, with no motives of self-interest, but with the sole desire to help humanity."

Mildred Lande, C.M.
Past President of the Auxiliary

about Chaki

Yehouda Chaki, an Israeli artist, born in Athens, Greece, in 1938, has lived in Montreal Quebec (Canada) since 1963. He studied under professor Joseph Schwartzman and at the Avni Academy in Tel Aviv under Stematsky, Mokadi and Streichman, and went on to study at the École des Beaux-Arts in Paris.

Chaki has exhibited extensively in Canada and the United States, in cities such as Montreal, Toronto, Vancouver, New York, Boston and Palm Desert, in addition to exhibiting in Israel, Belgium and Norway. He has had more than 85 one-man shows and more than 300 group exhibitions. His work is in the permanent collections of more than 75 museums and corporations. Among these collections are the Montreal Museum of Fine Art; Musée D'art Contemporain de Montréal; Fort Lauderdale Museum, Florida; Eretz Israel Museum, Israel; Musée de Toulon, France; and the Museo de Arte Moderna in Rio de Janeiro, Brazil. His work is found in prestigious corporate collections such as the Canadian embassy in Argentina, the Canadian consulate in New York, and the corporate collections of Coca-Cola Limited, Husky Oil and Gaz Metropolitain.

financial donors

one cup
Mildred Lande, C.M.
The Cons Family

tablespoon
Ernst & Young LLP

teaspoon
Joelle Berdugo-Adler, Diesel Canada
Robbie Spector, Banker's Pen (1991)
Emballages C&C Packing
Geoffrey J. Gelber, Gelmont Foundation
Todd and Shawna Sone and Family
Pharmascience Inc.
Matthew and Elana Poplaw and Family
Richter Charitable Foundation
Michael and Leslie Spector-Cons

handful
Steve Myro

scoop
Bessner Gallay Kreisman
Jerry and Louise Boman and Family
Jeffrey and Hela Boro
Avi and Ronit Jacobson
Standard Products
Richard Stern

recipe donors

The Panache team would like to thank all the chefs of Montreal for sharing their prized recipes and making this collection complete. Unfortunately, we were unable to include all of them. We apologize to those donors whom we may inadvertently have missed.

a Tina Abbey, Ronit Amsel, Beverlee Ashmele, Louis-Philippe Audette, Yvonne Azuelos | **b** Rachel Bacher, Ruth Ballon, Gloria Bass, Debbie Becker-Newpol, Dana Bell, Dahlia Ben-Dat Fisher, Luna Bendayan, Carol Berall, Arlene Berg, Barbara Berlin, Etty Bienstock, Mia Billick, Colleen Bismuth, Sylvie Bismuth, Annetta Black-Rotchin, Barbara Blauer, Allison Boman, Louise Boman, Hela Boro, Regine Bouadana, Stephen Bronfman, Heather Browman, Paula Brown, Bernice Brownstein, Cheryl Brownstein-Stein, Julie Brownstein | **c** Dana Caplan, Shari Chankowsky-Rotholz, Aidel Chanowitz, Edie Chernoff, Sherrie Child, Gail Cohen, Leonard Cohen, Maia Cooper, Felicia Cukier, Cummings Jewish Centre for Seniors Craft Centre | **d** Deborah Davis, Rona Davis, Theresa Dennill, Philippe De Vienne Traiteur, Howard Dubrovsky, Tina Dubrovsky, Tracy Dulas, Rhoda Durbin | **e** Mark Eiley, Yael Elfassy, Rosetta Elkins, Alicia Epstein, Lisa Epstein, Jennifer Exum | **f** Osnat Feldman, Leslie Fenster-Szirt, Ferreira Café Trattoria, Franceen Finesilver, Naomi Finkelstein, Rita Finestone, Audrey Finkelstein, Peggy Fixman, Lisa Flam, Eileen Fleischer, Elana Fogel-Poplaw, Jackie Freedman, Simone Friedman | **g** Iselott Gasman, Carole Gilman, Elaine Goldstein, Rachel Goodman, Rosalind Goodman, Shawna Goodman-Sone, Rhoda Granatstein, Kay Gray, Charlotte Guttman | **h** Esther Hajeman, Rena Helfenbaum, Wendy Helfenbaum, Dodo Heppner, Linda Hodess-Johnston, Annetta Hoffman, Ruth Horwitz, Andrea Howick, Stephanie Hutman-Glazer | **j** Maxine Jacobson, Nathalie Jarvis | **k** Stephanie Kapusta-Schipper, Phyllis Karper, Paula Kerllenevitch, Merle Klam, George Kopanis, Shirley Kornitzer, Carole Kosters, Fran Krane,

Robyn Krane, Tracy Kravitz, Elinor Kushansky | l Cheryl Lacey, L'Altro Restaurant, Philippe Laloux, Mildred Lande, George Lau, Maureen Leaman, Harvey Leavitt, Lianne Leboff, Bunny Lechter, Heather Leckner, John Ledwell, Angela Lehrer, Millie Lev, Janis Levine, Alta Levenson, Gertie Levine, Susan Levinger, Miriam Liberman, Donna Litvack, Jewel Lowenstein | m James Macguire, Melissa Margles, Sandy Martz, Julia Mauer, Carolyn Melmed, Mia Melmed-Goodman, Perla Meyers, Rona Miller, Dr. Fred Muroff | o Liz Orolowitz, Deborah Oshrega | p Elizabeth Perez, Pepino Perri, Sheila Pinsler, Rhoda Pinsky, Jane Plotnick, Jennifer Postelnik, Phyllis Postelnik | q Shoshana Quint | r Alice Raby, Stephanie Raby-Naimer, Suzy Ratner-Lourie, Chava Respitz, Restaurant Bice, Restaurant Matteo, Restaurant Primo & Secondo, Eve Rochman, Rachel Rochman, Tali Rochman, Penny Rudnikoff | s Beverly Salomon, Nora and Sylvie Salvaggio, Flora Sasportas, Risa Scherzer, Lori Schick, Sylvia Schneiderman, M. Schwartz, Julie Sckolnick-Garfield, Flora Shapiro, Monica Shapiro, Terry Sheiner, Simone Shouela, Jennifer Silver-Zangwill, Lily Sirikittikul, Wendy Sirota-Goldstein, Lisa Smith, S. Smoke, Virginia Sokoloff, Sheila Sone, Carole Spector, Leslie Spector-Cons, Barbara Stern | u Evy Uditsky, Jo-Anne Uditsky | v Rhoda Vineberg, Vinnie Gambinis Restaurant, Mario Vissa | w Margo Wexler, Randa Wexler, Meryl Witkin, Karen Worsoff | y Lili Yesovitch | z Susan Zangwill, Dana Zinman-Lohner, Andrea Zlotnik-Mendel

recipe testers

starters
Randa Wexler—Chair

Ronit Amsel, Arlene Berg, Hela Boro, Iselott Gasman, Linda Hodess-Johnston,
Sheila Notkin, Joanna Ruckenstein

soups
Dahlia Ben-Dat Fisher—Chair
Roz Rinzler—Chair

Nathalie Batshaw, Jacob Bratin, Sherri Bratin, Arie Fisher, Lisa Hamaoui, Debbie Honigwachs,
Aviva Kalin, Stephanie Kapusta-Schipper, Katie Keri, Samara Kornitzer, Aviva Miller, Adina Moss,
Manny Moss, Sara Rinzler, Virginia Sokoloff, Stephanie Tordjman

salads
Stephanie Hutman-Glazer—Chair
Robyn Krane—Chair

Ilana Baranoff, Monique Bensadon, Lisa Brookman, Penny Cohen, Karen Forman,
Romy Hutman-Schick, Marcie Krane, Lysa Lash, Donna Litvack, Wendy Nadler, Deborah Ohnona,
Zena Rosenberg, Sari Sacks, Frances Sigal, Leslie Spector-Cons

breakfast & brunch
Lianne Routtenberg—Chair
Andrea Zlotnick-Mendel—Chair

Sylvie Bismuth, Gail Cohen, Amy Fish, Adele Friedman, Miryam Fruchtermann, Marjorie Heft,
Mia Melmed-Goodman, Renee Perlman, Alana Shiveck, Selena Smith, Marian Sniatowsky

poultry
Melissa Margles—Chair

Ronit Amsel, Etty Bienstock, Louise Boman, Mandy Ephraim-Steinberg, Leslie Fabian,
Iselott Gasman, Judi Hagshi, Harvey Leavitt, Tracey Lohner-Kravitz, Sara Rak,
Sandie Sparkman, Stephanie Steinman, Ronit Yarosky, Dana Zinman-Lohner

meat
Ronit Amsel—Chair

Sylvie Bismuth, Sherrie Child, Iselott Gasman, Rosalind Goodman, Shawna Goodman-Sone,
Rosalie Gordon, Dr. Avi Jacobson, Maxine Jacobson, Melissa Margles, Julie Matlin,
Shoshana Quint, Rachel Shanfield, Dr. Issie Shanfield, Stephanie Steinman

fish
Julie Brownstein—Chair
Eve Rochman—Chair

Sylvie Bismuth, Randi Eiley, Rachel Rochman, Tali Rochman, Leslie Szirt, Lucy Wolkove

vegetarian
Howard Dubrovsky—Chair
Joanna Yufe-Naimer—Chair

Jennifer Croll-Wolfe, Sharyn Katsof-Coviensky, Angela Lehrer, Stephanie Raby-Naimer, Lisa Singer-Miller

on the side
Tania Guindi—Chair

Elana Fogel-Poplaw, Nathalie Gabbay, Julie Miller, Heidi Minkoff,
Galit Mizrahi, Tiffany Pinchuk, Lesli Sheinberg-Winkler

desserts | bars & cookies
Julie Brownstein—Chair
Mark Eiley—Chair

Gloria Bass, Monique Bensadon, Nathalie Celenecki-Lang, Danielle Elmaleh-Schafer,
Mandy Ephraim-Steinberg, Karen Forman, Simone Friedman, Stephanie Hutman-Glazer, Elana Green,
Ann Hoffman, Lindsay Holesh-Stark, Marlene King, Robyn Krane, Tamara Leighton, Susan Levinger,
Samantha Mintz-Vineberg, Joanna Naimer, Deborah Ohnona, Alice Raby, Stephanie Raby-Naimer,
Sari Sacks, Jennifer Silver-Zangwill, Robyn Singerman, Alissa Sklar, Sharon Steinberg,
Stephanie Steinman, Elana Tafler, Lena Weinberger, Randa Wexler, Andrea Yampolsky

cookbook team

consultants

Sandra Agulnik, Arlene Berg, Karen Etingin, Susie Fishbein, Norene Gilletz,
Doron Goldstein, Elaine Goldstein, Rosalie Gordon, Rhoda Granatstein, Leonard Greenfield,
J&R Butcher, Harvey Leavitt, Carol Lesser, Marsha Rosen, Judy Shaikovitch, Lucy Wolkove

editing

Arlene Berg, Hela Boro, Dana Caplan, Deborah Davis, Karen Etingin, Eileen Fleischer,
Rosalind Goodman, Shawna Goodman-Sone, Rhoda Granatstein, Stephanie Hutman-Glazer,
Merle Klam, Robyn Krane, Doree Levine, Mia Melmed-Goodman, Stephanie Raby-Naimer,
Jennifer Silver-Zangwill, Virginia Sokoloff, Leslie Spector-Cons, Randa Wexler, Dana Zinman-Lohner

fundraising

Shawna Goodman-Sone—Chair

Ronit Amsel, Louise Boman, Eliza Buksbaum, Yael Elfassy, Rosalind Goodman,
Melissa Margles, Rochelle Sochaczevski, Leslie Spector-Cons

cooking classes

Yael Elfassy—Chair

Ronit Amsel, Yvonne Azuelos, Susan Balinsky, Gloria Bass, Julie Brownstein, Sherrie Child,
Randi Cola, Elaine Dubrovsky, Howard Dubrovsky, Rosalind Goodman, Sharyn Katsof-Coviensky,
Merle Klam, Susan Levinger, Elizabeth and Norman Lum, Melissa Margles, Gideon Pollack,
Shoshana Quint, Sylvia Quint, Stephanie Raby-Naimer, Robyn Singerman,
Marylin Takefman-Backman, Randa Wexler, Dana Zinman-Lohner

marketing and sales

Allison Boman—Chair

Valerie Abitbol, Ronit Amsel, Daniella Assaraf, Sylvie Bismuth, Robyn Krane, Stephanie Hutman-Glazer,
Angela Lehrer, Doree Levine, Donna Litvack, Lisa Rubin, Ellen Teitelbaum, Alyssa Wolfe

photography | illustrations

Jonathan Ross Goodman | Lisa Lipari

pantry notes

how to use this book

- Always read through a recipe completely before starting.
- If you are cooking with metric measurements, please note that they are approximate.
- Throughout the cookbook you will notice symbols at the top of the page to make your recipe selection easier.

  F = FREEZES **D** = DAIRY **M** = MEAT **P** = PAREVE

- Vegetable stock can be substituted for chicken stock to make recipes pareve. Conversely, chicken stock can be substituted for vegetable stock in other recipes.

- When using vegetable stock, we prefer the Tetra Pak versions that are made with organic vegetables and are free of MSG.

- Many of the recipes in the book can be used during Passover.

- To ensure the best flavour, **always start with the freshest ingredients**—fresh or frozen vegetables, fresh fish and meats from reliable grocers and spices that are restocked at least once a year.

- Remember—**quality in, quality out!** Store spices in the freezer to extend their shelf life and to preserve freshness.

- Spanish onions are a good all-purpose onion for cooking.

- Sugar refers to granulated sugar unless otherwise noted.

- Kosher salt is preferred for cooking for its purity and coarse texture.

- 1 lemon yields 1 teaspoon (5 mL) of zest and 3–4 tablespoons (45–60 mL) of juice.

- 1 clove garlic equals 1 teaspoon (5 mL) minced garlic.

notes on oil

- Oil can refer to canola, vegetable, safflower or grapeseed oil. Try to use monounsaturated oils like canola and olive oil, which are good for your health.

- Reserve extra-virgin olive oil for salads, marinades and as a condiment to appreciate its cold pressed fruity olive flavour.

dairy notes

- In our recipes, the butter we call for is *always* unsalted. Salt is a preservative and masks staleness.

- Unless otherwise noted, margarine can be substituted for butter to make recipes dairy free.

- One stick of butter equals ½ cup (125 mL).

- Buttermilk can easily be made at home. Add 1 tablespoon (15 mL) lemon juice or vinegar to 1 cup (250 mL) milk. Let curdle for 2 minutes before using.

- If a dairy-free alternative is desired for regular milk, replace it with soy milk or rice milk in your cooking and baking.

- Milk can be frozen for up to three weeks although some separation may occur after thawing. Shake thawed milk well before serving or using in cooking or baking.

- Half-and-half cream is ½ cream and ½ milk and contains about 11 percent fat.

- Heavy cream contains roughly 35 percent fat.

- Whipping cream can replace heavy cream.

- Our recipes always call for large eggs. 1 egg equals 2 egg whites or ¼ cup (60 mL) egg substitute.

- 5 extra-large eggs equal about 6 large eggs.

notes on breading, baking, flour . . .

- Matzo meal can be used in place of flour for breading.

- 1 tablespoon (15 mL) cornstarch equals 1 tablespoon (15 mL) potato starch.

- 1 cup (250 mL) all-purpose flour equals ¼ cup (60 mL) matzo cake meal plus ¾ cup (180 mL) potato starch sifted together.

- ½ cup (125 mL) all-purpose flour equals 2 tablespoons (30 mL) matzo cake meal plus 6 tablespoons (90 mL) potato starch.

- Self-rising flour contains 1 teaspoon (5 mL) baking powder and ½ teaspoon (2 mL) salt per cup (250 mL) of flour.

- 1 ounce (25 g) unsweetened chocolate equals 3 tablespoons (45 mL) cocoa plus 1 tablespoon (15 mL) unsalted butter or margarine.

- Confectioner's sugar is the same as icing and powdered sugar.

- 1 cup (250 mL) dark brown sugar can be replaced with 1 cup (250 mL) white sugar plus ¼ cup (60 mL) unsulphured molasses.

notes on safe thawing

- There are three safe ways to thaw food: 1) in the refrigerator, 2) in cold water, or 3) in the microwave. It's best to plan ahead for slow, safe thawing in the refrigerator.

- Small items may thaw overnight; most foods require a day or two. Large items like turkeys may take longer—one day for each 5 pounds of weight.

- For faster thawing, place food in a leak-proof plastic bag and immerse it in cold water. If the bag leaks, bacteria from the air or surrounding environment could be introduced into the food. Check the water frequently to be sure it stays cold. Change the water every 30 minutes. After thawing, refrigerate the food until ready to use.

- When microwave-thawing food, plan to cook it immediately after thawing because some areas of the food may become warm and begin to cook during microwaving.

- Keeping partially cooked food for use later is not recommended, as bacteria may be present.

roasted vegetables 101

- Count on 1½–2 pounds (750g–1 kg) of vegetables for 4 people.

- The smaller the pieces, the faster the cooking time.

- Try to cut vegetables into equal-sized pieces so that the cooking time is the same for all.

- Make sure vegetables are in 1 layer; otherwise they will steam and not roast. Use more than 1 baking sheet if necessary.

- Stir vegetables periodically while roasting. If roasting more than one kind of vegetable, remove those that are ready and continue roasting the rest.

- Toss the vegetables with olive oil, kosher salt and freshly ground pepper (optional) before roasting.

- Flavour with fresh or dry herbs such as thyme, rosemary, chili flakes or other spices, or with balsamic vinegar for some taste variety.

Vegetable	Preparation	Oven temperature	Cooking time
Beets	Peeled, sliced	425°F (220°C)	30–45 minutes
Brussels sprouts	Trimmed, left whole	400°F (200°C)	35 minutes
Carrots	Peeled, thickly sliced	425°F (220°C)	30–45 minutes
Cherry tomatoes	Whole	400°F (200°C)	15–20 minutes
Eggplant	Chunks	425°F (220°C)	30–45 minutes
Fennel	Sliced or halved lengthwise	425°F (220°C)	30–45 minutes
Green beans	Whole	425°F (220°C)	20 minutes
Onions	Cut in half, sliced in wedges	425°F (220°C)	30–45 minutes
Parsnips	Peeled, thickly sliced	425°F (220°C)	30–45 minutes
Peppers	Halved	425°F (220°C)	30–45 minutes
Potatoes and sweet potatoes, winter squash	Unpeeled, wedges or quarters	425°F (220°C)	30–45 minutes
Zucchini	½- to 1-inch (1–2.5-cm) slices	425°F (220°C)	20 minutes

suggested menus

SUNDAY BRUNCH
Montreal Big Orange
Whipped Smoothie, 101

Frittata with Feta, Sun-Dried
tomatoes and Basil, 97

Market Salad with
Honey Garlic Dressing, 71

Rebetzin's Coffee Cake, 92

BACKYARD BBQ
Pearl Barley Salad with
Roasted Red Bell Peppers
and Smoked Mozzarella, 78

Grilled Cedar-Planked Salmon, 137

Oven-Roasted Asparagus, 168

Grilled Pineapple with
Caramel Sauce, 191

WINTER WONDERLAND
Eggplant Caponata, 28
with Pita Chips, 31

Corn Chowder with Wild Rice, 52

Curried Lamb with Apricots, 126

Molten Chocolate Cakes, 196
with Raspberry Coulis, 208

SPRING LUNCH
Bruschetta with Ricotta
and Artichoke Hearts, 33

St. Tropez Salad, 68

Sea Bass en Papillote, 142

Rice with Vermicelli,
Green Onions and Garlic, 180

Zesty Lemon Squares, 215

AUTUMN DINNER PARTY
Roasted Butternut Squash
and Apple Soup, 56

Chicken Breasts with
Cranberries and Pine Nuts, 105

Apple Berry Crisp with
Oatmeal Streusel Topping, 194

PASSOVER
Carrot and Sweet Potato Soup
with Fresh Thyme, 51

Baked Gefilte Fish Loaf, 147

Chicken Piccata, 106

Flourless Chocolate-Orange
Almond Cake, 197

SUMMER BUFFET LUNCH
Fattoush, 64

Fasoulia, 161

Fresh Corn Spoon Bread, 155

Rustic Plum Galette, 192

Triple Chocolate
Fudge Brownies, 216

VEGETARIAN DINNER
Marinated Goat Cheese
Rounds, 29

Cream of Asparagus Soup , 48

Moroccan Tagine
with Chickpeas, 152

Poached Pears, 203
with Caramel Sauce, 191

starters

Previous page: Marinated Goat Cheese Rounds

Dukka

MAKES: 4 CUPS (1 L)

Dukka's origin is Egyptian but now it is a popular companion to a glass of wine. A great party dish that brings guests together! This recipe halves easily for smaller gatherings, or keep half to give as a hostess gift. It can be kept in the refrigerator for up to one week, or frozen for up to six months.

Preheat oven to 350°F (180°C).

Line a rimmed baking sheet with aluminum foil. Lay the macadamia nuts or cashew nuts, hazelnuts and sunflower seeds on the sheet and bake for 7 minutes.

Remove from the oven and sprinkle with coconut. Return to the oven and bake until fragrant and golden brown, about 2 minutes more. Watch carefully because coconut tends to burn quickly. Cool. Remove from the baking sheet and set aside.

Using the same baking sheet, toast the sesame seeds, coriander seeds and cumin seeds, shaking occasionally, until the sesame seeds are golden, about 8 minutes. Watch carefully so that they do not burn. Cool.

Place the seed mixture in a food processor bowl and pulse until finely chopped. Add nuts and pulse until fairly smooth, leaving some texture. Add the seasonings and stir to blend to produce the dukka.

To serve, cut or tear the pita into small pieces. Dip in oil and then in the dukka.

Variation: May be served with hummus instead of oil for dipping.

Freezing: Freeze in a well-sealed container for up to a year.

½ cup (125 mL) macadamia or cashew nuts

¼ cup (60 mL) hazelnuts

¼ cup (60 mL) sunflower seeds

¼ cup (60 mL) unsweetened shredded coconut

1 cup (250 mL) sesame seeds

½ cup (125 mL) coriander seeds

¼ cup (60 mL) cumin seeds

1 teaspoon (5 mL) kosher salt

1 teaspoon (5 mL) ground cumin

½ teaspoon (2 mL) freshly ground pepper

½ teaspoon (2 mL) cinnamon

¼ teaspoon (1 mL) cayenne pepper

soft thick fresh pita rounds

extra-virgin olive oil

D

Tzatziki

MAKES: 1½ CUPS (375 mL)

A flavourful and refreshing low-fat dip, topping or spread. Teamed with pita bread chips this is an easy starter. By drawing the liquid from the yogurt, we are left with a pressed yogurt cheese that is rich in flavour without the added calories.

2 cups (500 mL) plain yogurt

1 medium English cucumber, peeled and grated

1 teaspoon (5 mL) kosher salt

2 cloves garlic, minced

2 tablespoons (30 mL) extra-virgin olive oil

1 tablespoon (15 mL) chopped fresh dill

2 teaspoons (10 mL) white wine vinegar

½ teaspoon (2 mL) freshly ground pepper

Spoon the yogurt into a sieve lined with a coffee filter or cheesecloth. Set the sieve over a bowl and refrigerate, covered, for about 5 hours, or overnight, until the volume of yogurt is reduced to about 1⅓ cups (325 mL). Discard any liquid from the bowl and set the yogurt aside.

Put the cucumber in a clean sieve set over a bowl and sprinkle with salt. Let drain at room temperature for 1 hour and then squeeze excess liquid from the cucumber.

Combine the yogurt, cucumber, garlic, oil, dill, vinegar and pepper. Mix until well combined. Taste and season with more salt and pepper if necessary.

Cover and refrigerate before serving.

Guacamole

(P)

MAKES: 2 CUPS (500 mL)

Botanically a fruit, avocados can be prepared both in a sweet or savoury fashion. When shopping for avocados, look for them to yield slightly when lightly pressed.

Use a fork to mash the avocado lightly. Add the tomato, red onion, cilantro and lime. Keep it chunky! Season to taste with salt and pepper.

If making in advance, mash and add avocado just before serving. Or wrap tightly in plastic wrap to prevent air from coming in.

Variation: If you are short of tomatoes, add 2 tablespoons (60 mL) of prepared salsa.

3 ripe avocados
1 ripe tomato, chopped
½ small red onion, chopped
handful of cilantro, chopped
juice of ½ lime
kosher salt
freshly ground pepper

Eggplant Caponata

MAKES: 4 CUPS (1 L)

A Sicilian tomato-based eggplant salad that is great when guests drop over for a glass of wine, served with fresh halved mini pitas or Pita Chips (see page 31).

1–1¼ pounds (500–625 g) eggplant

⅓ cup (75 mL) olive oil

1 medium onion, chopped

⅓ cup (75 mL) chopped green bell pepper

8 ounces (250 g) mushrooms, chopped

2 cloves garlic, chopped

1 teaspoon (5 mL) kosher salt

½ teaspoon (2 mL) dry oregano

½ teaspoon (2 mL) freshly ground black pepper

5½ ounce (156 mL) can tomato paste

¼ cup (60 mL) water

2 teaspoons (10 mL) red wine vinegar

½ cup (125 mL) pimento-stuffed green olives, chopped

3 tablespoons (45 mL) pine nuts

¼ cup (60 mL) rinsed and drained capers

Cut the eggplant, keeping the skin on, into ½-inch (1-cm) cubes. Heat the oil in a large sauté pan over medium heat, then cook the eggplant, onion, green pepper, mushrooms and garlic for 15 to 20 minutes, stirring occasionally.

Add the salt, oregano, pepper, tomato paste, water, vinegar, olives, pine nuts and capers. Reduce the heat to low and simmer, covered, for 25 minutes or until all the vegetables are soft.

Refrigerate until ready to serve.

Chef's tip | THE FLAVOUR IMPROVES IF PREPARED AT LEAST 1 DAY AHEAD. SERVE AT ROOM TEMPERATURE.

Marinated Goat Cheese Rounds

SERVES: 4

A few simple ingredients that come together to create a unique taste. Try adding the goat cheese (chèvre) to a mix of baby greens for a light lunch.

Use dental floss to slice the goat cheese into ¾-inch (2-cm) rounds and place them close together, lying flat, in a shallow serving dish.

Whisk together the remaining ingredients and pour over the cheese. Cover with plastic wrap and refrigerate overnight or up to 1 week before serving.

Bring to room temperature before serving. Serve with fresh baguette slices.

Chef's tip | IT IS EASIER TO CUT THE GOAT CHEESE WHEN IT IS VERY COLD—THE FLOSS CUTS THROUGH CLEANLY.

1 6-ounce (175-g) log soft goat cheese (chèvre)

⅓ cup (75 mL) extra-virgin olive oil

3 tablespoons (45 mL) balsamic vinegar

½ clove garlic, finely minced

1 tablespoon (15 mL) fresh thyme, finely chopped

1 teaspoon (5 mL) coarsely ground peppercorns

10 kalamata olives, pitted and finely chopped

1 teaspoon (5 mL) freshly grated lemon zest

Fig and Walnut Tapenade with Goat Cheese

MAKES: 2 CUPS (500 mL)

This tapenade is a great variation on the Provençal classic that is often served as a condiment or with crudités. Figs are an ancient symbol of peace and prosperity. The tapenade can be prepared up to 3 days ahead. Bring to room temperature before serving.

1 cup (250 mL) dried figs, stemmed and chopped

⅓ cup (75 mL) water

⅓ cup (75 mL) kalamata olives, chopped

2 tablespoons (30 mL) extra-virgin olive oil

1 tablespoon (15 mL) balsamic vinegar

1 tablespoon (15 mL) capers, drained and chopped

¾ cup (185 mL) walnuts, toasted and chopped

1½ teaspoons (7 mL) fresh thyme, chopped

kosher salt to taste

freshly ground pepper

1 10-ounce (300-g) log soft fresh goat cheese (chèvre)

fresh thyme sprigs, for garnish, optional

In a heavy medium-sized saucepan, combine the figs and water. Cook over medium-high heat until all the liquid evaporates and the figs are soft, about 7 minutes. Transfer to a medium-sized bowl.

Add the olives, oil, vinegar, capers, ½ cup (125 mL) walnuts and chopped thyme. Stir to combine. Season with salt and pepper to taste.

Cut the cheese crosswise into ½-inch (1-cm) rounds (see Chef's tip, page 29). Arrange on a large serving platter, overlapping the rounds in a circle.

Spoon the mixture into the centre of the cheese circle.

Garnish with ¼ cup (60 mL) walnut halves and thyme sprigs, and serve with your favourite breads or crackers.

Pita Chips

(P)

MAKES: 8 DOZEN

These pita chips can be prepared and frozen in a plastic container for a couple of weeks or kept at room temperature for one week.

Preheat oven to 350°F (180°C).

Using scissors or a sharp knife, cut around the outside edge of each pita and separate it into two circles. Cut each circle into 8 triangles.

Place the triangles on baking sheets and use a pastry brush to brush lightly with olive oil. Sprinkle with garlic powder, paprika, salt, rosemary, oregano and basil.

Bake for 5 to 7 minutes, or until crisp. Cool the pita chips before storing to prevent steaming.

Variation: Use flour tortillas instead of pita bread.

6 8-inch (20-cm) pitas
1 tablespoon (15 mL) olive oil or olive oil spray
garlic powder
paprika
kosher salt
dry rosemary
dry oregano
dry basil

Challah Crisps

MAKES: 7 DOZEN

A great way to make use of leftover challah. These crisps are crunchy and highly addictive.

1 loaf unsliced square challah, crust removed

6 tablespoons (90 mL) unsalted butter, melted

2 tablespoons (30 mL) sesame seeds

1 tablespoon (15 mL) poppy seeds

2 tablespoons (30 mL) dry onion flakes

3 tablespoons (45 mL) grated Parmesan cheese

1 tablespoon (15 mL) powdered garlic

1½ teaspoons (7 mL) kosher salt

1 teaspoon (5 mL) freshly ground pepper

Preheat oven to 400°F (200°C).

Line a baking sheet with aluminum foil.

Cut the bread lengthwise into ½-inch (1-cm) thick slices. Lay the slices flat, cut them into ½-inch (1-cm) wide strips, then cut the strips in half crosswise. Place the bread sticks on the baking sheet and brush with butter.

Combine the sesame seeds, poppy seeds, onion flakes, Parmesan, garlic, salt and pepper in a bowl. Sprinkle the seed mixture over the bread, pressing slightly into the bread so it sticks.

Bake for 7–8 minutes. Turn over and bake for 4–5 minutes more until golden brown.

Serve warm or at room temperature.

Bruschetta with Ricotta
and Artichoke Hearts

ⓓ

SERVES: 6–8

From the Italian word bruscare, *to roast over coals. Do not assemble the bruschetta too far in advance or the toast will get soggy and lose its crunch.*

Preheat broiler.

Blend the cheese, oil, salt and pepper until smooth.

For the artichoke topping, heat the oil over medium heat in a medium-sized skillet. Add the garlic and cook for 1 minute. Be careful not to burn the garlic. Add the artichoke hearts and sauté until warm, about 4 minutes. Season with salt and pepper.

To assemble, place the bread slices on an ungreased baking sheet and toast in batches, about 3 inches (7.5 cm) from the heat, for about 1 minute on each side or until golden. Transfer the toasted bread slices to a work surface. Spread with the seasoned ricotta then add the artichoke topping.

Garnish with chopped parsley, Parmesan and freshly ground black pepper, and serve immediately.

CHEESE
½ cup (125 mL) ricotta cheese

1–2 tablespoons (15–30 mL) olive oil

kosher salt

freshly ground pepper

ARTICHOKE TOPPING
1–2 teaspoons (5–10 mL) olive oil

1–2 cloves garlic, minced

1 14-ounce (398-mL) can artichoke hearts, drained, quartered

kosher salt

freshly ground pepper

1 baguette, sliced diagonally ½ inch (1 cm) thick

GARNISH
1–2 tablespoons (15–30 mL) chopped fresh flat-leaf parsley

1–2 tablespoons (15–30 mL) grated Parmesan cheese

freshly ground pepper

Mushroom Phyllo Triangles

F D

Serves: 8

A wonderful rich savoury filling wrapped in a paper-thin crispy shell. Phyllo dough is extremely versatile and can be shaped in a multitude of ways. Work quickly when handling phyllo because it tends to dry out. The mushroom filling makes 4 cups (1 L), enough for 16 triangles.

MUSHROOM FILLING

3 tablespoons (45 mL) unsalted butter

2 pounds (1 kg) fresh mushrooms, sliced

¼ cup (60 mL) chopped onion

1 tablespoon (15 mL) vermouth or dry white wine

1 teaspoon (5 mL) kosher salt

4 ounces (125 g) cream cheese, at room temperature, cut into small pieces

1 cup (250 mL) fine fresh bread crumbs

½ cup (125 mL) plain yogurt

½ cup (125 mL) sour cream

⅓ cup (75 mL) chopped fresh flat-leaf parsley

2 large cloves garlic, minced

2 teaspoons (10 mL) fresh lemon juice

½ teaspoon (2 mL) freshly ground pepper

TRIANGLES

18 sheets frozen phyllo pastry, thawed

½ cup (125 mL) melted unsalted butter or olive oil

For the mushroom filling, melt the butter in a 12-inch (30-cm) skillet over medium-high heat. Add the mushrooms and onion and sauté, stirring frequently, until golden and the mushroom liquid has reduced. Stir in the vermouth or white wine and the salt and cook until the alcohol has evaporated.

Remove from the heat and drain well through a fine meshed sieve. Return the mushroom mixture to the pan.

Add the cream cheese to the mushrooms and stir until melted. Place over low heat if necessary. Add the bread crumbs, yogurt, sour cream, parsley, garlic, lemon juice and pepper, and mix until well combined. Cool. Refrigerate until ready to use. The filling can be prepared 2 days ahead or frozen for up to one month. Thaw in the refrigerator before using.

Preheat oven to 375°F (190°C). Line a baking sheet with parchment paper. Unfold phyllo dough on the counter.

For the triangles, quickly cover the phyllo with 2 overlapping sheets of plastic wrap and then a dampened kitchen towel to prevent it from drying out. Lay out 1 sheet of phyllo with its long side parallel to the edge of the counter and brush it lightly with melted butter. Place a second sheet of phyllo on top of the first and brush with melted butter. Repeat for a total of 3 sheets.

Cut the sheets crosswise through all 3 layers into 4-inch (10-cm) strips. You will have 3 or 4 strips depending on the length of the sheet.

Place ¼ cup (60 mL) of filling at the bottom of each strip. Fold 1 corner of the pastry diagonally over the filling to the opposite edge to form a triangle. Continue to fold the triangle onto itself, as if folding a flag, right to the end of the pastry strip. Place the triangles on the prepared baking sheet, seam side down, and ½ inch (1 cm) apart. Brush the outside of each triangle with melted butter.

Bake for about 15 minutes or until golden.

Freezing: Triangles can be prepared and flash frozen on a baking sheet until solid and then stored between sheets of waxed paper in a plastic container for up to 3 months. Bake while still frozen for about 20 minutes until golden.

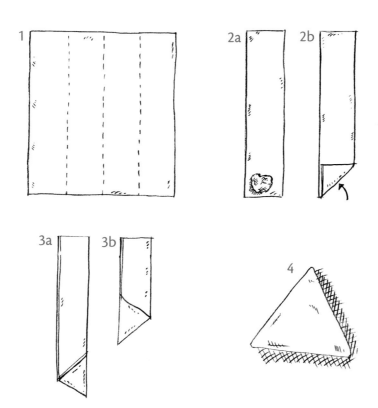

Tortillas with Caramelized Pears and Goat Cheese

MAKES: 24 ROUNDS

A fabulous juxtaposition of sweet caramel and savoury goat cheese. A great make-ahead hors d'oeuvre that is novel and simple to prepare. The tortilla rounds can be used to hold any of your favourite dips.

1 package flour tortillas (about 8)

¼ cup (60 mL) unsalted butter

½ cup (125 mL) sugar

2 firm pears, cut into small dice

2 ounces (50 g) goat cheese, crumbled

2 tablespoons (30 mL) fresh basil, chiffonade (see Chef's tip), for garnish

Using a 2–3 inch round cookie cutter, cut the tortillas into small rounds. Set them aside.

Preheat oven to 400°F (200°C).

In a small nonstick skillet on high heat, heat the butter and sugar. Stir. When the sugar begins to dissolve and darken, after about 5 minutes, add the diced pears. Do not be alarmed when the caramel seizes and hardens. Keep stirring, and it will melt again and caramelize. Cook until the mixture is soft but not mushy, about 7 minutes. Set aside to cool.

Place the tortilla rounds on a cookie sheet lined with parchment paper. Add small amounts of the goat cheese and top with the caramelized pears. Bake for 5 minutes.

Garnish with fresh basil chiffonade and serve immediately.

Chef's tips | A CHIFFONADE IS THIN STRIPS OR SHREDS OF VEGETABLES OR HERBS. TO CHOP, ROLL THE LEAVES OR BUNCH THE HERBS IN A MOUND AND SLICE FINELY.

FLOUR TORTILLA ROUNDS CAN BE FROZEN.

Seared Tuna on Wonton Crisp with Wasabi Cream

D

MAKES: 32 PIECES

Freshness and quality are key for this recipe. Make sure to use sushi grade tuna. The wonton squares may be prepared up to three days in advance.

For the wontons, add oil to a depth of 1 inch (2.5 cm) to a 2-quart (2 L) saucepan. Heat the oil until hot but not smoking.

Deep-fry 4 wonton squares at a time, turning once, for about 10 seconds. Drain on a plate lined with a paper towel. Repeat until all the squares are fried. Set aside.

For the wasabi cream, add the wasabi powder to the sour cream and mix well. Cover and refrigerate until needed.

Cut the tuna into ¾-inch (2-cm) strips. Set aside. The thickness of the tuna steak must be equal to the width of the strips so that the finished slices are square.

In a small shallow bowl, combine the white and black sesame seeds.

Generously brush each tuna strip on all 4 sides with sesame oil. Season with salt and pepper. Dip the tuna strip in the sesame seeds, coating all 4 sides. Repeat with the remaining strips.

Heat a nonstick skillet over medium-high heat until hot. Sear three tuna strips at a time on all 4 sides, for 20 seconds per side.

To assemble, cut each strip into ½-inch (1-cm) slices. Place each slice of tuna, rare side up, on a wonton square. Top with a tiny dollop of wasabi cream and some chives.

WONTONS

vegetable oil for deep-frying

8 square wonton skins, thawed and cut into 4 equal squares

WASABI CREAM

1 tablespoon (15 mL) wasabi powder

¼ cup (60 mL) sour cream

TUNA

1 tuna steak about ½ pound (250 g), and ¾ inch (2 cm) thick, about 4 x 5 inches (10 x 12 cm) wide

¼ cup (60 mL) white sesame seeds

¼ cup (60 mL) black sesame seeds

2 tablespoons (30 mL) toasted sesame oil

kosher salt

freshly ground pepper

snipped fresh chives, for garnish

Baked Phyllo Chicken Spring Rolls

Ⓕ Ⓜ

MAKES: 30 ROLLS

Traditional spring rolls in a new light wrapper that eliminates frying. Serve with Spicy Sesame Ginger Sauce (see page 41) or store-bought hoisin sauce. Make smaller rolls for bite-sized enjoyment. Spring rolls can be made ahead of time, covered with a damp towel and refrigerated until ready to bake.

1 tablespoon (15 mL) vegetable oil

2 medium onions, diced

1 pound (500 g) ground chicken

3 cloves garlic, minced

1 cup (250 mL) bean sprouts

½ cup (125 mL) halved and thinly sliced (lengthwise) green beans

1 cup (250 mL) thinly sliced cabbage,

1 cup (250 mL) shredded carrots

½ cup (125 mL) sliced green onions, white and green parts

2 tablespoons (30 mL) soy sauce

½ teaspoon (2 mL) sugar

2 teaspoons (10 mL) chopped fresh basil

2 teaspoons (10 mL) minced fresh ginger

½–1 teaspoon (2–5 mL) chili paste

kosher salt to taste

freshly ground pepper to taste

15 frozen phyllo sheets, thawed

½ cup (125 mL) melted pareve margarine, or olive oil

In a large skillet over medium-high heat, heat oil and sauté the onions until soft. Add the chicken and garlic and continue to cook until there are no signs of pink in the meat and almost all the moisture has evaporated. Stir during browning to break up pieces of chicken.

Add the bean sprouts, green beans, cabbage, carrots and green onions and sauté until wilted, about 3 minutes. Add the soy sauce, sugar, basil, ginger, chili paste, salt and pepper. Mix well and cool.

Cut the phyllo sheets in half crosswise. Place 1 sheet on a flat surface. Keep the remaining sheets covered with plastic wrap and a damp towel to prevent the pastry from drying out.

Lightly brush the phyllo sheet with melted margarine or oil. Place about 1½ tablespoons (22 mL) of the chicken mixture in the centre of one short end of the phyllo. Fold over twice to enclose the filling. Fold both sides in and continue rolling to form a neat cylinder. Place seam side down on a greased baking sheet. Brush the roll with more margarine or oil and sprinkle with sesame seeds. Repeat with the remaining phyllo and filling.

Preheat oven to 375°F (190°C).

Bake for 10 to 15 minutes or until golden.

Variation: Substitute minced turkey, veal, veggie ground round or ground beef for chicken.

Freezing: Prepared rolls may be frozen on baking sheets and then stored in plastic containers for up to 3 months. Bake from frozen for 15 to 20 minutes until golden. Do not thaw or dough will get soggy.

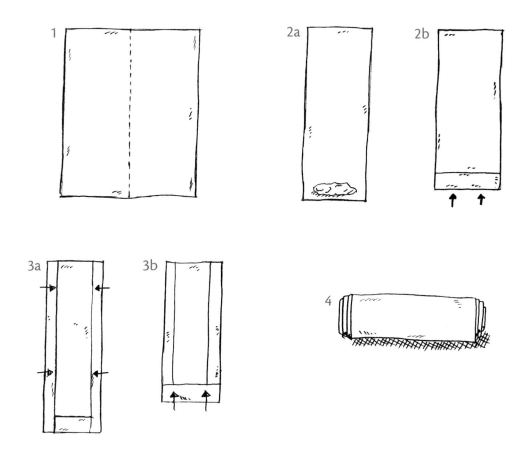

Steamed Wontons
with Spicy Sesame Ginger Sauce

MAKES: 72 DUMPLINGS

These are a crowd-pleaser because they are steamed instead of fried. Serve with a bowl of Spicy Sesame Ginger Sauce. Wontons, otherwise known as kreplach, also make a great addition to Chicken Soup (see page 47).

1–2 tablespoons (15–30 mL) vegetable oil

1 pound (500 g) mushrooms, finely chopped

2 large eggs

1 pound (500 g) ground chicken or turkey

4 green onions, white and green parts, finely chopped

2 tablespoons (30 mL) soy sauce

1½ tablespoons (22 mL) finely minced fresh ginger

2 cloves garlic, minced

1 package (72) frozen wonton wrappers, thawed

Heat oil in a large skillet over medium heat and sauté the mushrooms for about 10 minutes, or until cooked and liquid has evaporated. Set aside and cool slightly.

Beat the eggs in a large bowl. Add the chicken or turkey, green onions, soy sauce, ginger, garlic and sautéed mushrooms. Stir to combine.

To assemble, place 5 wonton wrappers on a clean work surface. Place 1 slightly rounded teaspoon (about 6 mL) of filling in the centre of each wrapper. Using your finger or a pastry brush, moisten the edges of the wrapper with water and fold each wrapper in half to form a triangle. Press the edges together to seal well.

Repeat with the remaining wrappers and filling. Place the prepared wontons on a greased baking sheet and flash freeze until solid. Package in a resealable plastic bag and store in the freezer until needed.

Place the wontons in a steamer on lettuce leaves or parchment to prevent sticking and steam for 10 minutes. Serve immediately with the sauce.

Spicy Sesame Ginger Sauce

MAKES: ½ CUP (125 ML)

𝒜 piquant accent to many Asian finger foods.

Combine the soy sauce, rice vinegar, sesame oil, chili paste, green onions, garlic, ginger and sugar and adjust to taste. This recipe can be doubled.

Store leftover sauce in a tightly sealed jar in the refrigerator for up to 1 week or in the freezer for up to 1 month.

¼ cup (60 mL) soy sauce

2 tablespoons (30 mL) rice vinegar

1 tablespoon (15 mL) toasted sesame oil

½ teaspoon (2 mL) chili paste

1 teaspoon (5 mL) minced green onions, white and green parts

1 clove garlic, minced

1 tablespoon (15 mL) finely minced fresh ginger

1–2 tablespoons (15–30 mL) sugar, to taste

Sushi Pizza

MAKES: 18 SQUARES

A superb example of fusion cuisine. To easily toast nori, bake it in a 300°F (150°C) oven for two to three minutes or toast both sides over a fire. When the nori is crisp and the colour has turned slightly green, it is done.

1 cup (250 mL) sushi rice

1⅓ cups (325 mL) water

2 tablespoons (30 mL) rice vinegar

scant 1 teaspoon (5 mL) sugar

½ teaspoon (2 mL) kosher salt

16 thin slices English cucumber

10 ounces (300 g) raw sushi grade salmon or tuna, thinly sliced, or smoked salmon

3 tablespoons (45 mL) mayonnaise

1½ teaspoons (22 mL) dry mustard

½ teaspoon (2 mL) wasabi powder

1 9 x 9-inch (23 x 23-cm) nori sheet, roasted

½–1 lemon, very thinly sliced

2 teaspoons (10 mL) sesame seeds, toasted

½ green onion, finely minced

Wash the sushi rice several times in lukewarm water until the water runs clear. Combine the rice with the 1⅓ cups (325 mL) of water in a saucepan and allow to rest, uncovered, for 30 minutes. Cook the rice covered in the soaking water over low heat until all the water is absorbed. Combine the vinegar, sugar and salt and stir to dissolve the sugar. Add the vinegar mixture into the hot cooked rice. Combine well. Place a dish towel over the saucepan and cool.

Meanwhile, line a 9 x 9-inch (23 x 23-cm) baking pan with 2 sheets of plastic wrap, crisscrossing each other and leaving a generous overhang on all 4 sides of the pan.

Place the cucumber slices, touching but not overlapping, in a pattern on the bottom of the pan. Lay the fish slices evenly over the cucumber.

Mix together the mayonnaise, dry mustard and wasabi powder and spread evenly over the fish. Spread half the cooked rice overtop and pack well. Place the nori sheet on top, then spread the remaining rice over the nori.

Cover with a sheet of plastic wrap, place a weight on top to pack down, then refrigerate for 30 minutes.

Invert the pizza onto a flat, preferably square, serving plate. Top with lemon slices and sprinkle with toasted sesame seeds and minced green onion.

Cut into 1½-inch (3.5-cm) squares to serve.

Chef's tip | COOKED SUSHI RICE ONLY LASTS FOR 1 DAY. IT CANNOT BE TREATED LIKE REGULAR LONG-GRAIN RICE, WHICH KEEPS IN THE REFRIGERATOR FOR UP TO 3 DAYS.

Caviar Pie

SERVES: 8–10

A sophisticated start to a delectable evening! Serve with pumpernickel bread, mini toasts or crudités.

Lightly butter an 8-inch (20-cm) springform pan.

Finely chop the eggs and mix with the mayonnaise. Season to taste with salt and pepper. Spread evenly over the bottom of the prepared pan. Scatter the onion evenly over the egg layer.

Beat the cream cheese with the sour cream and dill until smooth. Drop by spoonfuls over the onion and spread gently to cover the onion and egg completely. Cover and refrigerate for at least 3 hours or overnight.

Just before serving, spoon the caviar over the cheese layer. Garnish with a border of green onions and dill.

To serve, run a knife tip around the edge of the pie to loosen the sides. Gently release the ring and remove the pie. Set on a large serving plate.

Variations: Reduced-calorie versions of the mayonnaise, cream cheese and/or sour cream may be used.

Chef's tip | IF USING LUMPFISH CAVIAR, PLACE IT IN A SIEVE AND RINSE WITH COLD WATER TO REMOVE EXCESS COLOURING BEFORE USING.

6 large eggs, hard-boiled

2 tablespoons (30 mL) mayonnaise

kosher salt

freshly ground pepper

¾ cup (185 mL) very finely minced sweet white onion

8 ounces (250 g) cream cheese, softened

⅔ cup (150 mL) sour cream

2 tablespoons (30 mL) chopped fresh dill

2–3 ounces (50–75 g) black or lumpfish caviar

chopped green onions, white and green parts, for garnish, optional

chopped fresh dill, for garnish, optional

Grilled Baby Lamb Chops with Minted Vinegar Sauce

MAKES: 12 CHOPS

A dainty and sophisticated appetizer.

½ cup (125 mL) olive oil

¼ cup (60 mL) fresh rosemary

12 single tiny lean lamb chops
(2 pounds / 1 kg)

¼ cup (60 mL) packed brown sugar

¼ cup (60 mL) water

½ cup (125 mL) cider vinegar

½ cup (125 mL) apple jelly

½ cup (125 mL) chopped fresh mint

Combine the olive oil and rosemary and marinate the chops for 3–4 hours in the refrigerator.

Preheat broiler.

To make the sauce, combine the sugar, water and vinegar in a small saucepan and cook over medium heat until reduced by one-third. Add the apple jelly and heat thoroughly. Stir in the chopped mint just before serving so that it keep its colour.

Broil or grill the chops for 2–3 minutes on each side.

Serve immediately with the warm mint sauce as a dip on the side.

soups

Previous page: Tomato Soup with Spinach Pesto (top);
Corn Chowder with Wild Rice (middle); Fennel, Leek and Spinach Soup (bottom)

Chicken Soup

SERVES: 8

Nothing is more comforting than knowing you have a batch of homemade chicken soup, otherwise known as Jewish penicillin, in your freezer, ready to enrich many of your recipes! Keeping the skin on the onion gives a rich golden colour.

Place the chicken pieces in a large stockpot and cover with cold water. Bring to a boil and reduce to simmer. Skim the scum off the top of the soup. Cook for about 30 minutes to draw out the flavour.

Add the onion, leeks, carrots, celery, parsnips, peppercorns and bay leaves and simmer, partially covered, for about 2 hours, or until the chicken is tender and the vegetables are soft. Add the dill and parsley and continue cooking for another 20 minutes.

Remove the chicken and vegetables from the soup, and cool. Separate the chicken pieces, carrots and celery to be added back into the soup after straining. Strain the broth through a fine sieve lined with cheesecloth and chill overnight in the refrigerator. Use a large spoon to remove the layer of congealed fat the next day.

Warm the soup over medium heat. Season to taste with salt and pepper. (To use as a stock and not a finished soup, do not season with salt and pepper.)

Serve with diced chicken, noodles, vegetables and/or wontons.

Variations: To give your broth a golden colour and to add more nutrition, purée the carrots with 1 cup (250 mL) of stock. Slowly add it back to the broth until you reach the desired shade of gold for your broth. ♦ Use chicken and turkey bones instead of whole chicken. Make sure to include the necks!

Freezing: You can freeze stock in ice cube trays for up to 3 months.

1 5-pound (2.2-kg) chicken, skin included, cleaned, rinsed and cut up

14 cups (3.5 L) cold water

1 large onion, whole with skin

3 leeks, trimmed, white parts only, halved

4 peeled carrots, cut into chunks

3 stalks celery, cut into chunks

2 parsnips, cut into chunks

10 peppercorns

2 bay leaves

4–5 sprigs fresh dill

1 cup (250 mL) fresh flat-leaf parsley, stems included

kosher salt

freshly ground pepper

Cream of Asparagus Soup

SERVES: 4

A simple yet decadent soup, this recipe can be used as a template for making other creamy vegetable soups.

2 tablespoons (30 mL) unsalted butter

1 large onion, chopped

2 pounds (1 kg) asparagus, cut into ½-inch (1-cm) pieces

5–6 cups (1.25–1.5 L) vegetable stock

¼–½ cup (50–125 mL) heavy (35%) cream or milk

kosher salt

freshly ground pepper

In a 4-quart (4 L) heavy saucepan, melt the butter on medium heat. Add the onion and sauté until softened, about 4 minutes. Add the asparagus pieces and cook, stirring, for 5 minutes.

Add 5 cups (1.25 L) of stock and simmer, covered, until the asparagus pieces are very tender, 15–20 minutes. Purée the soup with a hand-held immersion blender or in batches in a blender and transfer to a bowl. (Always use caution when blending hot liquids.) Return to the pan and stir in the cream. Add more stock to thin the soup to the desired consistency if necessary. Do not let it boil.

Season with salt and pepper.

The soup may be prepared, covered and chilled 2 days ahead.

Variation: Try broccoli, parsnips, cauliflower, carrots, sweet potato or combinations of these instead of the asparagus.

Chef's tip | WHEN CHOOSING ASPARAGUS, LOOK FOR FIRM STALKS WITH TIGHTLY CLOSED BUDS. THE COLOUR SHOULD BE VIVID WITH NO SIGNS OF FADING. STORE THE ASPARAGUS STEMS UPRIGHT IN 1 INCH (2.5 CM) OF WATER AND USE WITHIN 2–3 DAYS. THEY LAST LONGER THIS WAY.

TO PREPARE ASPARAGUS: THE STALK WILL BREAK OR SNAP NATURALLY AT THE POINT WHERE IT STARTS TO GET TOUGH AND STRINGY. DISCARD THE LOWER PORTION OR RESERVE FOR STOCK.

Tomato Soup with Spinach Pesto

Ⓕ Ⓓ

This soup is a unique combination of ingredients and definitely worth the effort. A great soup to celebrate the end of summer! The tomatoes can be roasted 1 or 2 days ahead. The pesto can be prepared up to 2 days ahead.

Preheat oven to 425°F (220°C).

For the soup, place the tomato halves, cut sides up, on a rimmed parchment-lined baking sheet. Brush the cut tomato surfaces with the 1–2 tablespoons (15–30 mL) olive oil. Sprinkle with garlic, oregano and basil.

Bake until charred at the edges and beginning to shrivel (30–60 minutes), then scrape the tomatoes, oil and seasonings into a food processor. Process until 90% smooth, but with some pieces remaining.

Heat the 2 teaspoons (10 mL) olive oil in a large pot and sauté the onion until translucent. Add the wine and stock, bring to a boil and cook for 1 minute. Reduce heat and add the milk and ricotta and whisk until smooth. Add the tomato mixture. Stir to combine and heat thoroughly but *do not* allow to boil! Season with salt and pepper.

For the pesto, purée the spinach, salt, garlic, pine nuts and Parmesan in a food processor. Slowly pour the oil through the feed tube of the processor with the motor running to make a smooth pesto.

Serve the soup with a dollop of the pesto to add great flavour and colour.

Freezing: Freeze both soup and pesto separately.

SOUP

20 ripe plum (Roma) tomatoes, halved

1–2 tablespoons (15–30 mL) olive oil

3 garlic cloves, crushed

1–2 teaspoons (5–10 mL) dry oregano

1–2 teaspoons (5–10 mL) dry basil

2 teaspoons (10 mL) olive oil

1 medium onion, finely diced

½ cup (125 mL) red wine

2 cups (500 mL) vegetable stock

1 7-ounce (213-mL) can evaporated milk or ¾ cup (185 mL) whole milk

½ pound (250 g) ricotta cheese

¾ teaspoon (4 mL) kosher salt or to taste

freshly ground pepper

SPINACH PESTO

1 10-ounce (300-g) bag fresh spinach, cleaned and coarse stems removed

¼ teaspoon (1 mL) kosher salt

2 cloves garlic

1 cup (250 mL) pine nuts

1 cup (250 mL) grated Parmesan cheese

6 tablespoons (90 mL) olive oil

Fennel, Leek and Spinach Soup

SERVES: 6–8

A wonderful taste of spring! The longer you cook fennel, the less noticeable the anise (licorice) flavour becomes.

3 tablespoons (45 mL) olive oil

6 cups (1.5 L) chopped fresh fennel bulbs, stalks and fronds removed (set aside for garnish)

4 cups (1 L) chopped leek, white and pale green parts only

6 cups (1.5 L) chicken stock

⅔ cup (150 mL) packed spinach leaves, fresh or frozen

kosher salt

freshly ground pepper

Heat the oil in a large pot over medium heat. Add the fennel and leek and sauté until just translucent, about 15 minutes. Add the stock and cover. Simmer until the vegetables are tender, about 20 minutes.

Let the soup cool. Purée until smooth in small batches in a blender and transfer to a bowl, or use a hand-held immersion blender. Add the spinach to the last batch before puréeing.

Return the soup to the same pot and season with salt and pepper. Reheat the soup over low heat, stirring occasionally.

Ladle into bowls and garnish with the reserved fennel fronds before serving.

Chef's tip | FENNEL IS AN AROMATIC PLANT WITH A BULBOUS BASE, PALE GREEN STEMS AND BRIGHT FEATHERY TOPS THAT LOOK SIMILAR TO DILL. THESE WISPY TOPS, OFTEN CALLED FRONDS, CAN BE USED RAW AS A VIBRANT GARNISH.

Carrot and Sweet Potato Soup with Fresh Thyme

Ⓕ Ⓟ

SERVES: 6

A creamy puréed soup that is loaded with beta carotene. Save time by using two 1-pound (500-g) bags of peeled baby carrots.

In a soup pot, heat the olive oil. Sauté the onions for 5 minutes. Once the onions are translucent, add the minced garlic. Add the thyme, carrots, sweet potatoes, 5 cups (1.25 L) of stock, orange juice and bay leaf. Simmer partially covered until the vegetables are tender, 30–40 minutes.

Remove the bay leaf. Purée the soup in the pot with a hand-held immersion blender, or transfer to a blender and purée. If the soup is too thick, add more stock. Season to taste with salt and pepper.

Chef's tip | WHEN BLENDING HOT SOUPS IN A BLENDER, REMOVE THE CAP AND COVER THE JUG WITH A DISHTOWEL TO ALLOW STEAM TO ESCAPE. NEVER KEEP THE CAP ON OR IT WILL EXPLODE FROM THE PRESSURE OF THE STEAM.

1 teaspoon (5 mL) olive oil

1 red onion, chopped

2 cloves garlic, minced

1 teaspoon (5 mL) dry thyme or 1 tablespoon (15 mL) fresh thyme, chopped

2 pounds (1 kg) carrots, peeled and cut into chunks

2 medium sweet potatoes, peeled and cut into chunks

5–6 cups (1.25–1.5 L) vegetable stock

½ cup (125 mL) orange juice

1 bay leaf

kosher salt

freshly ground pepper

Corn Chowder with Wild Rice

SERVES: 8

A true harvest soup that celebrates corn and wild rice, two New World foods. The rich corn flavour is drawn from the sweet cobs of the corn. Wild rice is chewy and often pairs well with other grains to create interesting texture.

½ cup (125 mL) wild rice

2 teaspoons (10 mL) olive oil

1 onion, cut into small dice

2 cloves garlic, minced

1 carrot, cut into small dice

1 rib celery, chopped

8 ears fresh corn, kernels removed, cobs set aside (5 cups / 1.25 L fresh or frozen corn kernels)

1 Yukon gold potato, peeled and cubed

5–6 cups (1.25–1.5 L) vegetable stock

1 bay leaf

1 teaspoon (5 mL) kosher salt

freshly ground pepper

1 cup (250 mL) soy milk, optional

chopped fresh chives, for garnish, optional

In a small saucepan bring 4 cups (1 L) of water to a boil. Add the wild rice. Lower the heat to simmer and cook, covered, until soft, about 45 minutes. The rice will crack open. Drain, rinse and set aside.

In a large pot, heat the oil. Add the onion and sauté for 4 minutes until soft. Add the garlic, carrot and celery and sauté for another 3 minutes. Add 4 cups (1 L) of the corn, the potato, stock, bay leaf and corn cobs if using and continue to cook on medium-high heat, uncovered, for about 35 minutes or until the vegetables are soft.

Discard the bay leaf and cobs. Process the soup with a hand-held immersion blender right in the pot or transfer the soup to a blender. Purée until smooth.

Add the remaining cup (250 mL) of corn and the wild rice. Heat over medium heat until hot, stirring occasionally. Season the soup with salt and pepper. Adjust the consistency with an extra cup (250 mL) of stock or soy milk if using.

Garnish with chives, if using.

Variations: Try garnishing with chopped roasted peppers for contrasting colour. ◆ Add 1 cup (250 mL) of diced cooked Merquez sausage to add a smoky flavour and some protein to the soup.

Fresh Pea Soup
with Cardamom and Crème Fraîche

Ⓓ

SERVES: 4–6

*C*ardamom *is a spice often used in Indian cooking. It has warm flavours and is a member of the ginger family. This is a quick and easy soup that is ready in minutes!*

Heat the oil in a 3- to 4-quart (3–4 L) heavy saucepan. Add the onion and ginger and cook over medium heat, stirring occasionally, until the onion is softened, about 4 minutes. Add the cardamom and cook, stirring, for 30 seconds. Add the stock and bring to a boil. Add the peas and simmer, uncovered, until very tender, about 10 minutes.

Purée the soup in 3 batches in a blender until very smooth, at least 1 minute per batch (use caution when blending hot liquids). Transfer each batch to a bowl. Return to the pan, then season with salt and pepper and reheat.

Garnish with a dollop of crème fraîche.

Variation: Sour cream can be used instead of crème fraîche.

2 tablespoons (30 mL) olive oil
1 large onion, coarsely chopped
2 teaspoons (10 mL) minced peeled fresh ginger
¾ teaspoon (4 mL) ground cardamom
4 cups (1 L) vegetable stock
1 1-pound (500-g) package frozen peas
kosher salt
freshly ground pepper

Chef's tip | FOR MAXIMUM STRENGTH AND AROMA, GRIND YOUR OWN SPICES. TO GRIND, PLACE PODS IN A COFFEE GRINDER. GRIND UNTIL FINE.

Crème Fraîche

MAKES: 1 CUP (250 ML)

Stir the cream and buttermilk together in a bowl. Let stand for 24 hours in the refrigerator. It will stay fresh for 2 weeks, becoming increasingly thicker.

1 cup (250 mL) heavy (35%) cream
1 teaspoon (5 mL) buttermilk

Gazpacho

SERVES: 6–8

A Spanish favourite that is refreshing on a hot summer day. Try serving it in long-stemmed glasses for a dramatic effect. Preparing this a day ahead allows the flavours to develop to their fullest.

4 cloves garlic, minced

1 English cucumber, coarsely chopped

1 red bell pepper, coarsely chopped

1 red onion, peeled and coarsely chopped

6 ripe plum (Roma) tomatoes, seeded and coarsely chopped, or 1 28-ounce (796-mL) can diced tomatoes

1 19-ounce (540-mL) can tomato juice or tomato and vegetable juice

2 tablespoons (30 mL) chopped fresh basil

½ teaspoon (2 mL) chili powder

1 tablespoon (15 mL) fresh lemon juice

6 drops hot sauce

6 drops Worcestershire sauce

1–2 tablespoons (15–30 mL) extra-virgin olive oil

kosher salt

freshly ground pepper to taste

½ cup (125 mL) diced green onions, white and green parts, for garnish

1 avocado, diced

Process the garlic, cucumber, bell pepper, onion and tomatoes in a food processor until finely chopped. Transfer the vegetables to a large bowl and stir in the juice. Add the basil, chili powder, lemon juice, hot sauce, Worcestershire sauce and olive oil. Season to taste with salt and pepper.

Chill overnight. Garnish with diced green onions and avocado and serve with crusty bread.

Variation: If you opt to use vegetable juice, make sure to adjust the seasonings to compensate for the extra salt in the juice.

Chef's tips | WHEN SELECTING GARLIC, LOOK FOR BULBS THAT ARE FIRM, UNSPROUTED AND WELL WRAPPED IN WHITE OR MAUVE PARCHMENT-LIKE SKINS.

THE COLD TEMPERATURE OF THE SOUP CAN DULL THE FLAVOUR, SO MAXIMIZE THE USE OF SEASONINGS, INCLUDING HERBS AND SPICES.

Split Pea Soup with Fresh Dill

F P

SERVES: 6

A real French Canadian favourite without the meat! Split peas are a great pantry item to keep on hand for some low-fat protein in your diet. Small star noodles added at the end will provide extra body and texture to the finished soup.

In a large pot, heat the oil on medium heat and sauté the onion until translucent, about 4 minutes. Add the garlic and cook for another minute. Add the carrots, celery and parsnip and continue to sauté for 2 more minutes. Add the split peas, potatoes, stock or water and bay leaf. Bring to a boil, reduce the heat and simmer partially covered until the peas are soft and begin to break apart, about 1 hour.

Remove the bay leaf and purée the soup to the desired consistency. If it is too thick, add more stock or water. Add the dill and season with salt and pepper.

1 tablespoon (15 mL) olive oil

1 cup (250 mL) chopped onion

2 cloves garlic, minced

2 carrots, peeled and diced

2 celery stalks, diced

1 parsnip, peeled and diced

1 cup (250 mL) dried split peas, green or yellow, cleaned and rinsed

2 medium potatoes, peeled and diced

6 cups (1.5 L) vegetable stock

1 bay leaf

¼ cup (60 mL) chopped fresh dill

kosher salt

freshly ground pepper

Roasted Butternut Squash and Apple Soup

SERVES: 10

A creamy velvety soup that can be made with different types of winter squash like pumpkin, Hubbard and acorn. Serve in a hollowed-out pumpkin to give a tureen effect or carve out acorn squash for individual servings. Remember to keep the top to use as a cover to hold in the heat.

3 pounds (750 mL) butternut squash (1 large or 2 small squash)

1 tablespoon (15 mL) olive or vegetable oil

2 medium leeks, white parts only, cleaned and coarsely chopped (2 cups / 500 mL)

1½ tablespoons (22 mL) chopped fresh ginger

3 large Golden Delicious apples, peeled, cored and cut into eighths

5 cups (1–1.25 L) vegetable stock

½ cup (125 mL) unsweetened apple cider or apple juice

1 teaspoon (5 mL) kosher salt

½ teaspoon (2 mL) freshly ground pepper

½ cup (125 mL) half-and-half cream or soy milk, optional

Preheat oven to 400°F (200°C).

Cut the squash lengthwise and scoop out the seeds. Place cut side down on a baking sheet and roast in the oven until soft, about 1 hour. Cool. Scoop the flesh into a bowl and discard the skin.

In a large soup pot, heat the oil. Add the leeks and sauté for about 5 minutes on medium-high heat. Add the ginger and continue to sauté for 1 minute. Add the apples, squash, stock and cider or juice. Cook, covered, for about 20 minutes to meld.

Purée the soup with a hand-held immersion blender. If using a regular blender, purée the soup in small batches to prevent splattering, and return the puréed soup to the pot. The soup should be slightly sweet and thick.

Season with salt and pepper. Stir in the half-and-half or soy milk, if using. Do not let it boil.

Variation: Try adding 1 tablespoon (15mL) curry powder for an Indian twist!

Freezing: The squash flesh can be roasted in advance and frozen, sealed well in a container, for later use.

French Barley Soup

F D

Nothing is more comforting on a winter day than a warm bowl of barley soup. This soup is packed with flavour from the combination of caramelized onions and leeks. Top each bowl with a toasted crostini ("toasted bread" in Italian) and melted Gruyère cheese. This recipe doubles easily.

In a medium-size pot, heat oil on medium-low heat. Add the onion and sauté, stirring until golden, about 15 minutes.

Add the leeks and sauté for 3–4 minutes more. Add the ginger and cook for 1 minute longer. Add the barley and vegetable stock and bring to a boil. Reduce the heat, cover and simmer for 35–40 minutes until the barley is tender.

Stir in the soy sauce and pepper.

Ladle into bowls and sprinkle with cheese, if using, and chopped parsley.

Freezing: If after freezing the soup thickens, dilute it with more stock and adjust the seasonings.

2 tablespoons (30 mL) vegetable oil

1 large Spanish onion, quartered and thinly sliced

2 leeks, white parts only, thinly sliced

1 teaspoon (5 mL) grated fresh ginger

½ cup (125 mL) pearl barley

5 cups (1.25 L) vegetable stock

1–2 tablespoons (15–30 mL) soy sauce

freshly ground pepper to taste

½ cup (125 mL) Gruyère cheese, grated, optional

2 tablespoons (30 mL) chopped fresh flat-leaf parsley

Ⓕ Ⓜ

Red Lentil Soup with Curry

SERVES: 4–6

Red lentils, also called masur daal, *are bright reddish orange when raw and turn a beautiful shade of yellow when cooked. A fast and nutritious soup exploding with flavour! It can also be spooned over basmati rice for a satisfying vegetarian meal.*

1 teaspoon (5 mL) canola oil

1 cup (250 mL) chopped onions

2–3 cloves garlic, chopped

1 tablespoon (15 mL) curry powder

1 teaspoon (5 mL) cumin

pinch cayenne pepper

1½ cups (375 mL) red lentils, rinsed and picked over

6 cups (1.5 L) chicken stock

kosher salt

freshly ground pepper

juice of 1 lemon

chopped fresh flat-leaf parsley or cilantro, for garnish

In a large soup pot, heat the oil. Add the onions and sauté on medium-high heat for about 4 minutes or until translucent. Add the garlic and continue to sauté for 1 minute. Add the spices and sauté for another 30 seconds. The pan will be dry. *Do not panic!* Add the lentils and stock.

Bring to a boil and reduce the heat to medium. If the soup is foamy, skim the surface with a ladle. Cook until the lentils are soft and beginning to break apart, about 20–25 minutes.

Season with salt and pepper and add the lemon juice just before serving. Garnish with chopped parsley or cilantro.

Chef's tip | HEATING DRY SPICES HELPS TO BRING OUT THEIR FLAVOUR.

Pasta e Fagiole

SERVES: 4–6

A hearty Italian bean soup that varies from Mama to Mama. For more intense flavour, add a piece of Parmesan rind to the soup while it is cooking. Discard it after the soup has cooked.

In a large heavy soup pot, heat the oil. Add the onion and cook over medium heat for 4 minutes. Add the celery and carrot and continue cooking for 4 minutes. Add the chopped garlic and rosemary and cook for 1 minute. Stir in the tomatoes and 3 cups (750 mL) of stock and bring to a boil. Reduce the heat and simmer for 30 minutes, covered.

Add 2 cups (500 mL) of stock and the uncooked pasta. Simmer for about 8 minutes. Add the beans. Stir in the parsley and season to taste with salt and pepper. Add the spinach just before serving.

Serve and sprinkle with freshly grated Parmesan cheese.

Chef's tip | ONCE THE PASTA IS COOKED, THE SOUP WILL THICKEN. ADD MORE WATER OR STOCK, IF NEEDED, AND SEASON TO TASTE.

1 tablespoon (15 mL) olive oil

1 cup (250 mL) diced onion

1 stalk celery (½ cup / 125 mL), cut into small dice

1 medium-size carrot, cut into small dice (½ cup / 125 mL)

2 cloves garlic, finely chopped

1 teaspoon (5 mL) dry rosemary, chopped

2 cups (500 mL) diced peeled tomatoes

5–6 cups (1.5 L) vegetable stock, divided

1 cup (250 mL) small tubular pasta

½ cup (125 mL) cooked white cannellini beans, rinsed and drained

2 tablespoons (30 mL) chopped fresh flat-leaf parsley

½ teaspoon (2 mL) kosher salt

freshly ground pepper

1 cup (250 mL) loosely packed baby spinach

freshly grated Parmesan cheese

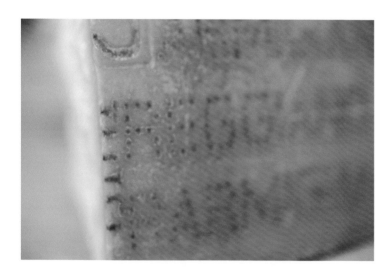

Previous page: Japanese Soba Noodles with Roasted Peppers and Shiitake Mushrooms

Tuscan Panzanella

SERVES: 4–6

This salad goes well with an Italian-themed meal. You must use good Italian or French bread— supermarket white bread will simply dissolve in the dressing. Serve the salad alongside or on top of breaded veal or grilled chicken to create an instant meal.

For the salad, combine the tomatoes, mixed baby greens, fresh basil and olives in a large salad bowl. Season with salt, pepper and oregano to taste.

For the dressing, combine the balsamic vinegar, lemon juice, oil, salt and pepper. Pour over the salad and top with the croutons just before serving.

Chef's tip | NEVER STORE TOMATOES IN THE REFRIGERATOR. LET THEM RIPEN ON THE COUNTER.

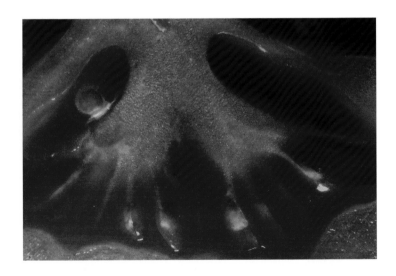

SALAD
8–10 plum (Roma) tomatoes, seeded and chopped into thick cubes

1 cup (250 mL) mixed baby greens

½–1 cup (125–250 mL) fresh basil leaves

½ cup (125 mL) kalamata olives, pitted and halved

kosher salt

freshly ground pepper

dry oregano

Croutons (see page 65)

DRESSING
6 tablespoons (90 mL) balsamic vinegar

1½ teaspoons (7 mL) fresh lemon juice

½ cup (125 mL) extra-virgin olive oil

kosher salt

freshly ground pepper to taste

Fattoush

SERVES: 6–8

A Lebanese bread salad that is packed with zest from fresh lemon juice and sumac, and crunch from baked pita chips. Sumac is a spice that is found in Middle Eastern grocery stores.

SALAD

2 large stale pita breads, torn into 1-inch (2.5-cm) pieces

1 medium English cucumber, seeded and cut into ½-inch (1-cm) cubes

1 pound (500 g) ripe tomatoes (about 3), seeded and cut into ½-inch (1-cm) cubes

6 green onions, both white and green parts, cut into ¼-inch (0.5-cm) slices

1 green bell pepper, cut into ½-inch (1-cm) cubes

¼ cup (60 mL) coarsely chopped fresh flat-leaf parsley

⅓ cup (75 mL) coarsely chopped fresh mint

3 tablespoons (45 mL) roughly chopped cilantro, optional

2 teaspoons (10 mL) sumac

LEMON DRESSING
MAKES: ½ CUP (125 mL)

2 cloves garlic, minced

¼ cup (60 mL) fresh lemon juice

⅓ cup (75 mL) extra-virgin olive oil

kosher salt

freshly ground black pepper

Preheat oven to 375°F (190°C).

For the salad, spread the pita pieces in a single layer on a large baking pan and bake until dry, about 10 minutes. Cool. This can be done 1 week in advance and the pita stored in a resealable bag.

In a large bowl combine the cucumber, tomatoes, green onions, green pepper, parsley, mint and cilantro, if using. Sprinkle with sumac. Set aside.

For the dressing, in a bowl, whisk together the garlic, lemon juice and olive oil. Season with salt and pepper to taste

Add the bread to the salad just before serving so that the bread does not become soggy. Toss the salad with the lemon dressing.

Chef's tips | ENGLISH CUCUMBERS (HOT HOUSE) CUSTOMARILY DO NOT NEED TO BE PEELED. TO ADD COLOUR, LEAVE SKIN ON THE WASHED CUCUMBER.

NEVER CHOP HERBS IN ADVANCE BECAUSE THEY WILL OXIDIZE AND TURN BLACK.

Caesar Salad

D

An egg-free version of the classic favourite enjoyed by everyone! You can make the croutons one week in advance and store. To add variety, try adding 8 ounces (250 g) of cooked fusilli pasta to make a delicious pasta salad.

For the dressing, mix together the water, sour cream, oil, sugar, vinegar, garlic, lemon juice, salt, pepper, Parmesan and horseradish. Refrigerate until needed. It will keep for 1 week.

Preheat oven to 350°F (180°C).

For the croutons, in a small skillet heat the oil. Add the garlic and sauté for 1 minute to infuse the flavour.

In a large bowl, toss the bread cubes with the flavoured oil. Spread them on a baking sheet and bake on the middle rack of the oven for 12–15 minutes or until dry and golden.

Just before serving, gently toss the romaine, grated Parmesan and croutons. Slowly add the dressing to taste. Garnish with Parmesan curls.

Chef's tips | THIS IS A GREAT OPPORTUNITY TO USE UP ANY LEFTOVER BREAD. CROUTONS CAN BE SEASONED WITH YOUR FAVOURITE HERBS!

TO PREPARE CURLS, MAKE SURE YOUR BLOCK OF CHEESE IS AT ROOM TEMPERATURE. USING A WIDE PEELER, DRAG YOUR PEELER ACROSS THE BLOCK TO CREATE CHEESE CURLS.

CAESAR DRESSING
MAKES: ABOUT 1 CUP (250 mL)

¼ cup (60 mL) water
½ cup (125 mL) light sour cream
¼ cup (60 mL) olive oil
¼ cup (60 mL) sugar
¼ cup (60 mL) white vinegar
3 cloves garlic, chopped
1 teaspoon (5 mL) fresh lemon juice
½ teaspoon (2 mL) kosher salt
1 teaspoon (5 mL) freshly ground pepper
¼ cup (60 mL) freshly grated Parmesan cheese
½ teaspoon (2 mL) prepared white horseradish

CROUTONS
2 tablespoons (30 mL) olive oil
1 teaspoon (5 mL) minced garlic
1 French baguette, cut into ½-inch (1-cm) cubes

SALAD
2 heads romaine lettuce, torn into bite-size pieces,
¼ cup (60 mL) freshly grated Parmesan cheese plus 6 ounces (175 g) Parmesan cheese at room temperature, shaved into curls, for garnish (see Chef's tip)

Greek Tomato and Onion Salad with Creamy Feta Dressing

SERVES: 4

Fill a warm pita with this enticing salad to be enjoyed on the run. The whipped dressing can also be used as a dip for crudités. Try mixing yellow and red tomatoes for a beautiful visual effect!

SALAD

2 large ripe tomatoes, sliced crosswise into ½-inch (1-cm) rounds

¼ medium red or Vidalia onion, thinly sliced into rounds

¼ cup (60 mL) kalamata olives, pitted and sliced

1–2 ounces (25–50 g) feta cheese, crumbled, for garnish

chopped fresh chives, for garnish

CREAMY FETA DRESSING
MAKES: ¼ CUP (60 mL)

1 ounce (25 g) feta cheese, crumbled

1½ tablespoons (22 mL) sour cream

1½ tablespoons (22 mL) water

1 tablespoon (15 mL) mayonnaise

2 teaspoons (10 mL) fresh lemon juice

1 teaspoon (5 mL) dry oregano

½ teaspoon (2 mL) minced garlic

¼ teaspoon (1 mL) freshly ground pepper

½ teaspoon (2 mL) kosher salt

For the salad, arrange the tomatoes on a serving platter and scatter the onions and olives overtop.

For the dressing, combine the feta, sour cream, water, mayonnaise, lemon juice, oregano and garlic in a food processor and process until smooth. Adjust seasonings to taste. Dressing will keep for 1 week in the refrigerator.

Drizzle the salad with the feta dressing before serving. Garnish with additional crumbled feta and chopped chives.

Variation: Use low-fat versions of the mayonnaise, sour cream and feta cheese to lower the fat content.

Chef's tips | FETA CHEESE CAN BE VERY SALTY SO ADJUST SEASONINGS ACCORDINGLY. IF TOO SALTY, SOAK FETA CHEESE IN WATER BEFORE ADDING TO THE RECIPE TO EXTRACT EXCESS SALT.

Roasted Portobello Mushrooms
on a Bed of Mesclun with Basil Vinaigrette

(P)

SERVES: 6

A sophisticated starter that is individually plated. Portobello mushrooms are overgrown cremini mushrooms that are meaty in texture and absorb flavour fully.

Preheat oven to 375°F (190°C).

Line a baking sheet with aluminum foil.

For the salad, use a teaspoon to scrape the gills from the underside of the mushrooms to prevent the salad from turning black. Brush the caps with oil and sprinkle with salt and pepper.

Place the mushrooms gill side down on a baking sheet. Roast for 15–20 minutes or until soft. Remove from the oven and slice into ½-inch (1-cm) slices.

For the dressing, combine the oil, balsamic vinegar, garlic, sugar, basil, lemon juice, salt and pepper in a sealed container. Shake well until blended.

Mix the salad greens and watercress, top with the sliced mushrooms and drizzle with the vinaigrette.

Chef's tip | DRESS LEAF SALAD RIGHT BEFORE SERVING TO RETAIN CRUNCH. ADD THE DRESSING GRADUALLY TO TASTE—DO NOT POUR IT ALL IN AT ONCE.

SALAD
6 large portobello mushroom caps

1 tablespoon (15 mL) olive oil

kosher salt

freshly ground pepper

1 pound (500 g) mesclun or other mixed greens

1 bunch watercress

BASIL VINAIGRETTE
MAKES: 1½ CUPS (375 mL)

1 cup (250 mL) olive oil

½ cup (125 mL) balsamic vinegar

1 garlic clove, minced

1 teaspoon (5 mL) sugar, to taste

1 cup (250 mL) fresh basil leaves, chopped

juice of 1 lemon

kosher salt

freshly ground pepper

St. Tropez Salad

SERVES: 6

A beautiful way to celebrate spring! Hearts of palm are a tasty pantry staple that can enrich many different salads in a pinch.

SALAD

2 pounds (1 kg) asparagus, trimmed, blanched and sliced 1 inch (2.5 cm) thick on a diagonal

1 14-ounce (398-g) can hearts of palm, drained and sliced 1 inch (2.5 cm) thick on a diagonal

2 cups (500 mL) cherry tomatoes, halved

1 avocado, cubed

DIJON-DILL DRESSING
MAKES: 2 CUPS (500 ML)

1 clove garlic, minced

2 teaspoons (10 mL) Dijon mustard

1 cup (250 mL) white wine vinegar

1 cup (250 mL) extra-virgin olive oil

4–5 sprigs of fresh dill

1 teaspoon (5 mL) sugar

½ teaspoon (2 mL) kosher salt

½ teaspoon (2 mL) freshly ground pepper

Combine the asparagus, hearts of palm and tomatoes in a large bowl.

In a blender or food processor, mix together the garlic, mustard, vinegar, oil, dill, sugar, salt and pepper. Refrigerate in a sealed container until needed.

Add the avocado and dressing just before serving to prevent browning of the avocado. Add the dressing slowly—you may not need it all.

Variation: Blanched green beans or snow peas, or a combination of both, can be used instead of asparagus.

Chef's tip | TO BLANCH VEGETABLES, IMMERSE THEM IN BOILING WATER FOR 1–3 MINUTES, DEPENDING ON THE THICKNESS OF THE VEGETABLE. DRAIN AND IMMERSE IN COLD WATER TO STOP THE COOKING PROCESS AND TO RETAIN COLOUR.

Shaved Fennel, Radish and Apple Salad with Lemon Vinaigrette and Parmesan

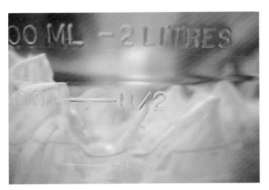

SERVES: 4–6

*F*ennel can be eaten cooked or raw and has a mild anise flavour. If you slice it in advance, squeeze fresh lemon juice on it to avoid browning. This is a great winter salad as an alternative to lettuce.

For the salad, bring the Parmesan cheese to room temperature. Place it on a cutting board. Run a wide peeler along the cheese to make Parmesan curls. Set aside for garnish.

Remove the stalks of the fennel and set aside the frilly fronds for garnish. Using the regular blade of a Japanese mandolin or a very sharp chef's knife, slice the fennel, apples and radishes finely and place in a serving bowl.

For the dressing, whisk the lemon juice and honey together in a bowl. Slowly whisk in the oil. Blend well. Season with salt and pepper.

Add the dressing to the salad and sprinkle with the crushed juniper berries, if using. Garnish with the Parmesan curls and fennel fronds.

Chef's tip | JUNIPER BERRIES HAVE A PUNGENT FLAVOUR AND NEED TO BE CRUSHED TO RELEASE IT. THEY ARE THE HALLMARK FLAVOURING OF GIN.

SALAD
1 6 x 2 x 1-inch (15 x 5 x 2.5-cm) block Parmesan cheese

2 fennel bulbs

1–2 firm apples such as Gala or Granny Smith

5 red radishes

2 tablespoons (30 mL) crushed juniper berries or ground red peppercorns, optional

LEMON VINAIGRETTE
MAKES: ABOUT 1 CUP (250 ML)

¼ cup (60 mL) fresh lemon juice

1 teaspoon (5 mL) honey

⅔ cup (150 mL) olive oil

kosher salt

freshly ground pepper

Spinach Salad
with Mangos and Candied Pecans

SERVES: 6

The candied pecans add interesting texture and flavour to this colourful salad. Look for Haas avocados, the brown pebbly skinned ones, which have the most flavour.

CANDIED PECANS
¼ cup (60 mL) packed brown sugar

1 tablespoon (15 mL) olive oil

1 tablespoon (15 mL) balsamic vinegar

¾ cup (185 mL) pecan halves

SALAD
2 6-ounce (175-g) bags or 5–6 cups (1.5 L) baby spinach, washed and dried

1 mango, peeled and cubed

¼–½ small red onion, thinly sliced

1 avocado, cubed

BALSAMIC DRESSING
MAKES: ½ CUP (125 mL)

2 cloves garlic, minced

1½ tablespoons (22 mL) Dijon mustard

3 tablespoons (45 mL) balsamic vinegar

¼ cup (60 mL) orange juice

2 tablespoons (30 mL) olive oil

kosher salt

freshly ground pepper

Line a baking sheet with aluminum foil.

For the candied pecans, bring the brown sugar, oil and vinegar to a boil in a small saucepan. Boil until the sugar dissolves. Add the pecans and stir. Remove from heat and immediately pour the pecans onto the baking sheet to cool. Break the pecans into pieces.

For the salad, combine the spinach, mango and onion in a large bowl.

For the dressing, whisk the garlic, Dijon mustard, balsamic vinegar, juice and olive oil together. Add salt and pepper to taste. Store in a tightly sealed jar in the refrigerator for up to 2 weeks.

Just before serving, add the cooled candied pecans and avocado to the salad ingredients and mix with dressing to taste (there will be some left over).

Chef's tips | CANDIED PECANS CAN BE STORED IN THE FREEZER IN AN AIRTIGHT BAG FOR UP TO 2 WEEKS.

TO RIPEN AVOCADOS QUICKLY, PLACE THEM IN A CLOSED PAPER BAG IN A DARK SPOT.

Market Salad
with Honey Garlic Dressing

SERVES: 6

A hearty plated salad that has great crunch! Nuts and seeds in salads add interesting texture and nutrition at the same time. Always toast nuts to improve flavour and to maximize shelf life.

For the salad, divide the lettuce among 6 plates. Mound the carrots and cheese on top of the lettuce and sprinkle with the seeds and walnuts. Top with the apple slices.

For the dressing, drop the garlic through the feed tube of the food processor into the bowl while the motor is running. Process until minced.

Scrape down the bowl. Add the vinegar, juice, honey, mustard, oil, salt and pepper and blend well. Drizzle dressing over the salad to taste. There will be lots of dressing left over.

Store leftover dressing in a tightly sealed jar in the refrigerator for up to 1 week.

Chef's tip | ALWAYS WASH GREENS AND SPIN DRY IN A SALAD SPINNER. WET LETTUCE WILL DILUTE THE DRESSING. HANDLE THE LETTUCE GENTLY TO AVOID BRUISING THE LEAVES.

SALAD
1 romaine lettuce, washed, dried and torn into bite-size pieces

2 cups (500 mL) shredded carrots

1½ cups (375 mL) grated mozzarella cheese

½ cup (125 mL) unsalted sunflower seeds

¼–½ cup (60–125 mL) walnut halves, toasted

2 Macintosh apples, cored and sliced, skin on

HONEY GARLIC DRESSING
MAKES: ABOUT 4 CUPS (1 L)

2 cloves garlic, minced

1 cup (250 mL) apple cider vinegar

1 cup (250 mL) unsweetened apple juice

1 cup (250 mL) honey

1 teaspoon (5 mL) dry mustard

2 cups (500 mL) canola oil

½ teaspoon (2 mL) kosher salt

¼ teaspoon (1 mL) freshly ground pepper

Moroccan Carrot Salad

SERVES: 6–8

A traditional salad that is often found at falafel stands. Serve this salad along with fresh pita and hummus.

8–10 medium-sized carrots, peeled and sliced into ½-inch (1-cm) rounds

2–3 cloves garlic, minced

2 teaspoons (10 mL) fresh lemon juice, or to taste

2 tablespoons (30 mL) sunflower or canola oil

1 heaping teaspoon (5 mL) paprika

1 teaspoon (5 mL) cumin

¼ teaspoon (1 mL) kosher salt

2 tablespoons (30 mL) chopped fresh flat-leaf parsley or cilantro

Bring the carrot rounds to a boil in a large pot. Boil for about 5 minutes or until al dente. Drain and set aside.

Combine the garlic, lemon juice, sunflower or canola oil, paprika, cumin and salt in a small bowl. Combine the hot carrots with the garlic mixture, then chill until ready to serve. Garnish the carrots with parsley or cilantro.

Serve either at room temperature or cold.

Chef's tip | JUICING LEMONS: IN ORDER TO EXTRACT THE MOST JUICE FROM A LEMON, ROLL IT ON THE COUNTER FOR A COUPLE OF MINUTES OR SQUEEZE THE WHOLE LEMON IN YOUR HAND TO SOFTEN. YOU CAN ALSO PUT IT IN THE MICROWAVE FOR 20 SECONDS. CUT IN HALF AND USE A FORK TO HELP DRAW OUT THE JUICE FROM THE LEMON. STRAIN OUT THE SEEDS.

Summer Potato Salad
with Roasted Peppers

P

SERVES: 4

Any mixture of seasonal vegetables can be used in this very versatile recipe. Make sure you use new or waxy potatoes because they have more moisture and less starch. Do not worry if the skins fall off.

Bring a large pot of water to a boil. Add the potatoes and boil until fork tender, about 15–20 minutes, then drain.

Place the potatoes, onion, roasted peppers, peas, basil and chives in a large bowl.

For the dressing, combine the dressing ingredients in a screwtop jar. Drizzle over the salad while the potatoes are still warm and toss well to coat. Season to taste.

Serve warm or at room temperature.

Chef's tip | COLD PRESSED EXTRA-VIRGIN OLIVE OIL IS THE FINEST GRADE OF OLIVE OIL. FLAVOUR VARIES DEPENDING ON THE GROWING REGION AND TYPE OF OLIVE. RESERVE EXTRA-VIRGIN OLIVE OIL FOR COLD DISHES TO APPRECIATE AND SAVOUR THE FLAVOUR.

POTATO SALAD
2 pounds (1 kg) new red potatoes, washed and halved

¼ cup (60 mL) chopped red onion

2 red bell peppers, roasted and julienned

½ cup (125 mL) fresh peas, raw

¼ cup (60 mL) fresh basil, chiffonade

2 tablespoons (30 mL) chopped fresh chives

DRESSING
¼ cup (60 mL) balsamic vinegar

½ cup (125 mL) extra-virgin olive oil

kosher salt

freshly ground pepper

French Lentils
with Arugula and Goat Cheese

SERVES: 4–6

A delicious assembled salad that has a variety of textures and flavours. These small green lentils, called lentilles de Puy, *are firm and have an earthy flavour and take a touch longer to cook than brown lentils.*

LENTILS

8 ounces (250 g) French lentils
(de Puy)

3 cups (750 mL) vegetable stock

4 sprigs fresh thyme or ½ teaspoon
(2 mL) dry thyme

DRESSING

1 tablespoon (15 mL) red wine
vinegar

1 tablespoon (15 mL) balsamic
vinegar

2 tablespoons (30 mL) extra-virgin
olive oil

kosher salt

freshly ground pepper

SALAD

3 cups (750 mL) arugula, well
washed and dried

1 roasted red bell pepper, thinly
sliced

2–3 tablespoons (30–45 mL)
pine nuts, toasted

4 ounces (125 g) goat cheese,
crumbled

Remove any stones from the lentils, place in a sieve and rinse under running water.

In a medium saucepan, combine the lentils, stock and thyme and bring to a boil. Lower the heat and simmer uncovered until cooked, about 20 minutes. The lentils should be firm but soft inside. Drain but do not rinse.

For the dressing, whisk together the vinegars with the oil until well combined. Season with salt and pepper. Separate the dressing into 2 containers. Marinate the warm lentils in half of the dressing.

For the salad, toss the rest of the dressing with the arugula when ready to serve. Divide the arugula among 6 plates. Top with the lentils and decorate with roasted pepper and pine nuts. Crumble goat cheese on top. Serve with crusty bread.

Japanese Soba Noodles with Roasted Peppers and Shiitake Mushrooms

(P)

SERVES: 8

An interesting pasta dish made from buckwheat noodles that can be served warm or cold depending on the time of year. A complete meal when served with grilled Asian chicken or fish.

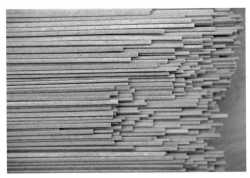

In a large stockpot bring 2 quarts (2 L) water to a boil and add the noodles. Cook according to the instructions on the package. Cooking times vary for different brands. Make sure not to overcook or the noodles will be too mealy. Drain, refresh under cold water to stop the cooking and drain again. Set aside.

For the dressing, whisk together the ginger, sesame oil, sugar, soy sauce and canola oil. Season to taste with salt and pepper.

Toss the noodles with the ginger dressing. Add the bell peppers, green onions and mushrooms and season with salt and pepper to taste. Garnish with the cilantro and sesame seeds.

Chef's tips | PLACE THE SESAME SEEDS ON A BAKING TRAY AND PLACE IN A 350°F (180°C) OVEN FOR ABOUT 5 MINUTES. WATCH CAREFULLY BECAUSE THEY BURN QUICKLY!

TO PEEL GINGER, SCRAPE AWAY THE PARCHMENT SKIN WITH THE BACK OF A TEASPOON. THERE IS NO NEED TO USE A PEELER, WHICH WILL OFTEN CAUSE A LOT OF UNNECESSARY WASTE.

SALAD

1 pound (500 g) dried buckwheat soba noodles or spaghetti

1 red bell pepper, roasted, peeled and julienned

1 yellow bell pepper, roasted, peeled and julienned

2 green onions, both green and white parts, cut on a diagonal into 1-inch (2.5-cm) pieces

10 fresh shiitake mushrooms, stems discarded, sliced

kosher salt

freshly ground pepper

10 sprigs fresh cilantro, coarsely chopped, for garnish

2–3 tablespoons (30–45 mL) sesame seeds, lightly toasted

GINGER DRESSING
MAKES: 1 CUP (250 mL)

½ teaspoon (2 mL) freshly grated ginger

1 tablespoon (15 mL) toasted sesame oil

2–4 tablespoons (30–60 mL) sugar, to taste

½ cup (125 mL) soy sauce

½ cup (125 mL) canola oil

kosher salt

freshly ground pepper

Salmon Seviche
with Lime Potato Pepper Salad

SERVES: 8

An unusually pretty first course with fresh flavours. Seviche is a Latin American raw fish salad. For all raw fish dishes, freshness of both the fish and the marinade is vital.

SALMON
1¼ pounds (625 g) centre-cut filleted fresh salmon (slightly less than 2 pounds / 1 kg before filleting)

kosher salt

freshly ground pepper

MARINADE
¾ cup (185 mL) fresh lime juice

6 tablespoons (90 mL) olive oil

2 jalapeño peppers, minced

2 cloves garlic, minced

1 stalk lemongrass, trimmed and minced

½ teaspoon (2 mL) kosher salt

¼ teaspoon (1 mL) freshly ground pepper

POTATO SALAD
1¼ pounds (625 g) tiny potatoes (grelots) or equivalent amount of red new potatoes, quartered

1 large red bell pepper, julienned

1 small green bell pepper, julienned

1 large yellow bell pepper, julienned

1 small red onion, thinly sliced

kosher salt

freshly ground pepper

¼–½ cup (60–125 mL) fresh cilantro, or to taste, chopped

2 small avocados, for garnish, quartered and sliced

Cut the salmon into paper-thin slices. Arrange decoratively in a large circle on 8 dinner plates. Cover each plate with plastic wrap. Stack the plates and chill until ready to serve. This can be prepared 1 day in advance.

For the marinade, combine the lime juice, olive oil, jalapeños, garlic, lemongrass, salt and pepper.

For the potato salad, cook the potatoes in salted water in a large pot until just tender. Drain the potatoes and toss with one-third of the marinade while still hot. Add the bell peppers and the onion. Adjust seasoning to taste. Toss the potato salad well and set aside.

To serve, drizzle marinade over the salmon to cover completely. Allow to stand for 12–15 minutes to "cook" the salmon. Season the salmon with kosher salt and pepper.

Toss the potato salad with the cilantro and mound in the centre of the salmon slices on each plate. Garnish with a fan of avocado slices and serve.

Chef's tip | LEMONGRASS IS AN HERB THAT LOOKS A BIT LIKE A PALE GREEN ONION EXCEPT THAT THE TOP AND OUTER LEAVES ARE TOUGH AND FIBROUS. USE ONLY THE TENDER BOTTOM PART. IT IS FOUND IN MOST SUPERMARKETS AND ASIAN MARKETS.

Couscous Salad with Roasted Chicken

Ⓜ

SERVES: 6–8

A colourful and refreshing salad full of fabulous fresh ingredients. This is a great way to use up leftover rotisserie chicken. The salad can be made 1 day in advance, covered and chilled until serving.

In a bowl, sprinkle the turmeric on the couscous to colour the grain. Boil the stock or water. Pour over the couscous and cover with a dish towel to steam. Let stand for 5 minutes. Fluff with a fork. Cool.

For the salad, mix the currants or cranberries, roasted peppers, chickpeas, green onions, cilantro and chicken with the couscous.

For the dressing, place the garlic, orange juice, balsamic vinegar, zest, cumin and oil in a blender. Blend well and season with salt and pepper to taste. The dressing can be stored in the refrigerator for up to 1 week.

Gradually pour the dressing over the salad and toss. Do not overdress or it will be soggy. Adjust seasonings.

To serve, line a large bowl with the romaine lettuce. Top with the salad.

Variation: Use flat-leaf parsley in place of the cilantro.

Chef's tips | SALADS ARE A WONDERFUL OPPORTUNITY TO BUILD A COMPLETE MEAL FROM LEFTOVERS. FOR INSTANCE, HARD-BOILED EGGS, COOKED RICE OR COUSCOUS ALONG WITH ALL SORTS OF COOKED FISH, CHICKEN OR MEAT HELP TO CREATE INTERESTING SALADS.

TURMERIC IS AN INDIAN SPICE DERIVED FROM A ROOT. IT GIVES A YELLOW/ORANGE COLOUR TO COOKED DISHES AND IS AN INEXPENSIVE SUBSTITUTE FOR SAFFRON. IT IS ONE OF THE MAIN INGREDIENTS IN CURRY POWDER.

COUSCOUS
½ teaspoon (2 mL) turmeric

3 cups (750 mL) couscous (2 10-ounce / 300-g boxes)

4½ cups (1.125 L) chicken stock

SALAD
1 cup (250 mL) dried currants or dried cranberries

1½ cups (375 mL) diced roasted red peppers

1 19-ounce (540-mL) can chickpeas, rinsed and drained

4 green onions, both white and green parts, thinly sliced

½ cup (125 mL) chopped fresh cilantro

1 3-pound (1.5-kg) roasted chicken, skinned, boned, cut into bite-size pieces

romaine lettuce leaves

ORANGE BALSAMIC DRESSING
MAKES: 1½ CUPS (375 mL)

1 clove garlic, minced

¾ cup (185 mL) orange juice

3 tablespoons (45 mL) balsamic vinegar

1 teaspoon (5 mL) freshly grated orange zest

1 teaspoon (5 mL) ground cumin

½ cup (125 mL) olive oil

½ teaspoon (2 mL) kosher salt

freshly ground pepper

Pearl Barley Salad with Roasted Red Bell Peppers and Smoked Mozzarella

SERVES: 6–8

A healthy and delicious salad to be served on its own or as a side dish. This perfect picnic salad is a tasty way to use barley and to increase the fibre in your diet. This salad can be assembled one day in advance without the herbs and dressing.

SALAD

2 cups (500 mL) pearl barley

1½ cups (375 mL) corn kernels, canned or frozen

1 small red onion, cut into small dice

6 green onions, both white and green parts, thinly sliced

2 roasted red bell peppers, cut into small dice

1 pint (500 mL) cherry tomatoes, quartered

1 small jalapeño pepper, finely minced

½ pound (250 g) smoked mozzarella, cut into small dice

½ cup (125 mL) chopped fresh flat-leaf parsley

½ cup (125 mL) chopped fresh basil

DRESSING

2 cloves garlic, minced

¼ cup (50 mL) balsamic vinegar

⅓ cup (75 mL) extra-virgin olive oil

kosher salt

freshly ground pepper

Rinse the barley twice under cold water to remove the starch. Half-fill a 3-quart (3 L) saucepan with water and add the barley. Bring to a boil, reduce the heat and simmer for 40–50 minutes until the barley is chewy. Drain and refresh with cold water.

If using canned corn, drain to remove liquid. Combine the vegetables and cheese. Add the cooked barley and chopped herbs.

For the dressing, whisk together the garlic and vinegar to blend well. Add the oil in a slow stream to create an emulsion. Season with salt and pepper.

Dress the salad 20 minutes before serving to allow the flavours to meld. Season to taste. Serve at room temperature.

Chef's tip | ROASTING PEPPERS: PLACE PEPPERS UNDER THE BROILER UNTIL THE SKINS BEGIN TO TURN BLACK. KEEP TURNING TO CHAR ALL SIDES. REMOVE FROM THE OVEN AND PLACE IN A PAPER BAG FOR 10 MINUTES. PEEL OFF THE SKIN AND REMOVE THE SEEDS. CHOP TO REQUIRED SIZE. NEVER RINSE A ROASTED PEPPER AS THIS WILL DECREASE THE FLAVOUR. ROAST A LARGE BATCH AT A TIME AND FREEZE THEM INDIVIDUALLY OR IN PAIRS FOR EASY USE THROUGHOUT THE YEAR.

Shanghai Beef Salad

Ⓜ

SERVES: 6–8

𝒜 perfect salad that can stand on its own as a meal. It is a wonderful opportunity to use leftover roast beef. Ginger has medicinal properties as well as being a seasoning agent. Fresh ginger steeped in tea is said to cure ailing stomachs, sore throats and coughs.

Combine the beef, spinach, mushrooms, bean sprouts, green onions, bell pepper, mandarin oranges and cashews in a large bowl.

For the dressing, combine the lemon juice, vinegar, soy sauce, honey, mustard, ginger, garlic, oil, salt and pepper. Toss with the salad just before serving.

Serve in a Chinese food take-out container for a fun picnic setting.

Chef's tip | BEEF IS EASIER TO SLICE WHEN COLD.

SALAD
4 cups (1 L) thinly sliced rare roast beef

4 cups (1 L) baby spinach

2 cups (500 mL) mushrooms, thinly sliced

2 cups (500 mL) bean sprouts, washed

2 green onions, both green and white parts, thinly sliced

1 red bell pepper, cut into strips

2 cups (500 mL) canned mandarin oranges, drained well

1 cup (250 mL) cashews, toasted

DRESSING
3 tablespoons (45 mL) fresh lemon juice

6 tablespoons (90 mL) cider vinegar

3 tablespoons (45 mL) soy sauce

2 tablespoons (30 mL) honey

1½ teaspoons (7 mL) dry mustard

1 tablespoon (15 mL) grated fresh ginger

3 cloves garlic, minced

¾ cup (185 mL) oil

kosher salt

freshly ground pepper to taste

Sweet Poppy Seed Vinaigrette

MAKES: 1¼ CUPS (300 ML)

This dressing goes well with baby spinach, chopped egg and mandarin oranges with slivered toasted almonds.

¼ cup (60 mL) chopped onion

1 clove garlic

1 tablespoon (15 mL) poppy seeds

1 tablespoon (15 mL) honey

⅓ cup (75 mL) rice wine vinegar

¼ cup (60 mL) apple cider
or apple juice

⅓ cup (75 mL) canola oil

½ teaspoon (2 mL) kosher salt

freshly ground pepper

Place the onion, garlic, poppy seeds, honey, vinegar, cider or juice, oil, salt and pepper in a food processor or blender and purée to combine. This dressing keeps refrigerated for up to 1 week.

Creamy Dill Dressing

MAKES: ABOUT 1½ CUPS (375 mL)

This whipped dressing is delicious on cold crunchy lettuce with cucumber, cherry tomatoes . . . any type of vegetable in fact! The secret to freshness is the fresh dill—it cannot be replaced with dried dill weed.

Combine the garlic, green onion, green pepper, vinegar, mayonnaise and fresh dill in a food processor. Process until smooth. Scrape down bowl.

Gradually add the oil through the feed tube while the motor is running. Season with salt and pepper to taste.

Refrigerate in a tightly sealed jar for up to 1 week.

2 cloves garlic, minced

1 green onion, both green and white parts

½ green bell pepper, seeded

½ cup (125 mL) red wine vinegar

3 tablespoons (45 mL) mayonnaise

2 tablespoons (30 mL) fresh dill

½ cup (125 mL) olive oil

½ teaspoon (2 mL) kosher salt

freshly ground pepper

Asian Vinaigrette

MAKES: 1 CUP (250 ML)

An easy zesty dressing that adds punch to any salad in seconds!

6 tablespoons (90 mL) white wine vinegar

5 teaspoons (25 mL) soy sauce or tamari (see Chef't tip)

2 cloves garlic, minced

1½ teaspoons (7 mL) sugar

½ teaspoon (2 mL) freshly ground pepper

½ teaspoon (2 mL) powdered ginger

½ cup (125 mL) safflower oil

Whisk together the vinegar, soy sauce, garlic, sugar, pepper and ginger in a bowl. Slowly add the oil in a stream to make an emulsion.

Store in a tightly sealed jar in the refrigerator for up to 1 week.

Chef's tip | TAMARI IS A JAPANESE SOY SAUCE. IT IS THICKER THAN REGULAR SOY SAUCE AND HAS A RICH, DEEP FLAVOUR.

breakfast & brunch

Previous page: Pecan Pumpkin Bread

Dutch Baby Pancake with Caramelized Apples

SERVES: 4–6

An oven-baked pancake that is sure to impress! A fast and easy dish with a custardy interior made from basic pantry ingredients that can be whipped together for an easy brunch.

Preheat oven to 425°F (220°C).

For the pancake, mix the milk, eggs, sugar and vanilla extract in a blender or food processor and blend thoroughly for 30 seconds at high speed.

When ready, add the flour and blend another 30 seconds to create a batter.

When the oven is hot, put the butter in a 10-inch (25-cm) cast iron skillet or ovenproof dish and place in the oven to heat.

When the butter has melted and is bubbling quickly, add the batter to the skillet. Bake for about 12–15 minutes or until the pancake has puffed and popped up over the edges of the pan and is golden brown.

For the topping, melt the butter and sugar in a medium-sized skillet. Add the apples and cinnamon and sauté on medium-high heat until soft.

Run a knife around the sides of the pan and slide onto a serving platter. Top with caramelized apples and sprinkle with some sifted confectioners' sugar. Cut into wedges.

Variation: Instead of apples, serve with warm maple syrup and fresh fruit.

PANCAKE
1 cup (250 mL) milk or soymilk

4 large eggs

1 tablespoon (15 mL) sugar

¼ teaspoon (1 mL) vanilla extract

1 cup (250 mL) all-purpose flour

2½ tablespoons (37 mL) unsalted butter

TOPPING
2 tablespoons (30 mL) unsalted butter

2 tablespoons (30 mL) sugar or maple syrup

2 Granny Smith apples, peeled and thinly sliced

pinch of cinnamon

confectioners' sugar, for garnish

Buttermilk Noodle Kugel

SERVES: 12

A light and comforting casserole that is welcome at any time of the year. The vanilla aroma will make your home smell heavenly! Serve with sour cream and fresh berries.

KUGEL
1 12-ounce (350-g) bag wide egg noodles

¼ cup (60 mL) unsalted sweet butter

4 large eggs, beaten

4 cups (1 L) buttermilk

½ cup (125 mL) sugar

1 teaspoon (5 mL) kosher salt

1 tablespoon (15 mL) vanilla extract

TOPPING
1 cup (250 mL) packed brown sugar

1 cup (250 mL) crushed corn flakes

2 tablespoons (30 mL) melted unsalted butter

Preheat oven to 350°F (180°C).

Lightly grease a 9 x 13-inch (3.5 L) baking dish.

For the kugel, cook and drain the noodles and transfer them to a very large bowl. Add the butter and stir through until melted.

In a separate large bowl, whisk together the eggs, buttermilk, sugar, salt and vanilla. Add the noodles and blend.

Transfer the noodle mixture to the greased baking dish and bake for 45 minutes.

For the topping, mix the brown sugar, corn flakes and butter together in a small bowl to make a crumb topping.

Remove the kugel from the oven and sprinkle the topping evenly over the top. Bake for an additional 30 minutes.

Remove from the oven and let stand for 10 minutes before serving.

Overnight French Toast with Blueberries

D

SERVES: 6–8

So simple to prepare and yet so delicious, friends will think you run a bed and breakfast in Vermont! Heat leftovers, if there are any, in the microwave.

For the caramel, bring the brown sugar, butter and cinnamon to a boil in a small saucepan and stir with a wooden spoon. Let boil for 2 minutes and turn off the heat. The caramel will be brown, thick and bubbly.

Drizzle the caramel evenly over the bottom of a 9 x 13-inch (3.5 L) baking dish. Cover with 6 slices of bread. Scatter the berries overtop. Place the remaining 6 slices of bread on the fruit.

For the custard, whisk together the eggs, milk, vanilla and salt in a medium-size bowl. Pour this evenly over the bread. Press down lightly with plastic wrap so that the bread absorbs the custard. Refrigerate overnight.

Preheat oven to 350°F (180°C).

Remove the plastic wrap and bake the French toast uncovered for 40–50 minutes until puffed and golden. Cut into squares, invert to show the caramel and place on a serving platter.

Variation: Sliced bananas, raspberries or a combination of both may be used instead of blueberries.

Chef's tip | TO CLEAN THE DRIED CARAMEL FROM THE POT, FILL THE POT WITH WATER AND BRING TO A SIMMER. LET SIT AND THEN CLEAN. RESIDUE WILL WASH AWAY QUICKLY.

CARAMEL
1 cup (250 mL) packed brown sugar

½ cup (125 mL) unsalted butter

1 teaspoon (5 mL) cinnamon, optional

TOAST
12 thick slices challah or brioche

1½ cups (375 mL) fresh or frozen blueberries or raspberries

CUSTARD
5 large eggs

1½ cups (375 mL) milk

1½ teaspoons (7 mL) vanilla extract

½ teaspoon (2 mL) salt

Sweet Cheese Pie
with Cornmeal Crust

SERVES: 8

Cornmeal creates a lovely yellow crust for this mildly sweet cheese pie. It makes a perfect buffet dish that can be prepared in advance and served with fresh raspberries and yogurt.

FILLING
1 pound (500 g) dry cottage cheese

⅓ cup (75 mL) sugar

1 teaspoon (5 mL) vanilla extract

2 large eggs, beaten

⅓ cup (75 mL) milk

BATTER
½ cup (125 mL) unsalted butter, melted

½ cup (125 mL) sugar

½ cup (125 mL) milk

1 large egg

½ cup (125 mL) all-purpose flour

½ cup (125 mL) cornmeal

2 teaspoons (10 mL) baking powder

Preheat oven to 325°F (160°C).

Lightly grease an 8-inch square (2 L) baking dish.

For the filling, mix together the cottage cheese, sugar, vanilla, eggs and milk in a large bowl. Set aside.

For the batter, whisk the butter, sugar, milk and egg together in a bowl. Add the flour, cornmeal and baking powder and stir until combined.

Pour half the batter into the greased baking dish. Cover with the cottage cheese filling and top with the remaining batter.

Bake for 1 hour. Serve warm.

Chef's tip | DRY COTTAGE CHEESE IS ALSO CALLED NO-CURD DRY COTTAGE CHEESE, PRESSED COTTAGE CHEESE OR HOOP CHEESE.

Apricot Orange Bread

F D

MAKES: 4 MINIATURE LOAVES OR 1 REGULAR SIZE LOAF

A sensational aroma that will fill your home with the fragrance of orange blossoms! A hearty flavourful loaf, low in fat, with interesting texture from the crunch of the nuts and the chewiness of the apricots.

Preheat oven to 350°F (180°C).

Lightly grease a 9 x 5-inch (2 L) loaf pan.

Place the apricots in a bowl and cover with 1 cup (250 mL) of boiling water. Let stand for 20 minutes to plump the apricots. Drain and reserve the soaking water from the apricots (about ⅓ cup / 75 mL). Add to the orange juice to make 1 cup (250 mL) of liquid.

Chop the apricots and combine with the orange zest.

In a large mixing bowl, cream the butter and sugar. Add the egg and vanilla and beat well. Add the juice mixture, then gently stir the flour, baking powder and salt into the liquid mixture. Mix until the flour disappears. The batter should be lumpy, so don't try to make it smooth. Stir in the apricots and nuts, if using.

Pour the batter into the prepared pan. Bake for about 25 minutes for small loaves or about 1 hour for a large loaf (or until a wooden pick inserted in the cake comes out dry). *Do not overbake!* Cool on a rack.

1 cup (250 mL) dried apricots

1 orange, juice and freshly grated zest

2 tablespoons (30 mL) unsalted butter or margarine, at room temperature

⅔ cup (150 mL) sugar

1 egg

1 teaspoon (5 mL) vanilla extract

2 cups (500 mL) all-purpose flour

2 teaspoons (10 mL) baking powder

pinch of salt

½ cup (125 mL) walnuts or pecans, toasted and chopped, optional

Banana Bread

MAKES: 2 LOAVES OR 3 DOZEN LARGE MUFFINS

A great way to use up ripe bananas. Store whole ripe, unpeeled bananas in the freezer and defrost in the microwave for 1 minute.

3¼ cups (800 mL) all-purpose flour

2 teaspoons (10 mL) baking soda

½ teaspoon (2 mL) cinnamon

½ teaspoon (2 mL) salt

4 large eggs, at room temperature

2⅓ cups (575 mL) sugar

1 cup (250 mL) vegetable oil

8 very ripe bananas, coarsely mashed (about 3 cups / 750 mL)

¼ cup (60 mL) sour cream or plain yogurt

2 teaspoons (10 mL) vanilla extract

1⅓ cups (325 mL) walnuts , toasted (see Chef's tip on page 153) and chopped

Preheat oven to 350°F (180°C).

Grease 2 loaf pans (each 9 x 5 inches / 2 L) and dust with flour.

In a bowl, whisk together the flour, baking soda, cinnamon and salt. Beat the eggs and sugar in a mixer at medium-high speed until very thick and lemon coloured (about 5 minutes). Reduce speed to low and slowly add the oil.

Mix in the mashed bananas, sour cream or yogurt and vanilla. Gently fold in the flour mixture. Stir in the nuts.

Bake the loaves for about 1 hour or until golden brown. For muffins, bake for 18 minutes for large and 12 minutes for small. Cool for 10 minutes on a baking rack before removing from pans.

Variation: Instead of walnuts, use 1 cup (250 mL) miniature chocolate chips.

Chef's tips | ALWAYS SET YOUR OVEN TIMER A COUPLE OF MINUTES BEFORE THE ALLOTTED BAKING TIME TO CHECK YOUR FOOD—DIFFERENT OVENS COOK AT DIFFERENT RATES.

NEVER CHOP NUTS WHEN THEY ARE STILL WARM. THEY WILL TURN INTO PASTE.

Pecan Pumpkin Bread

Ⓕ Ⓟ

MAKES: 2 LOAVES

Pumpkin, cinnamon and cloves have an affinity for each other. The pumpkin adds moisture and an autumnal hue to the loaf. Leftover canned pumpkin can be frozen.

Preheat oven to 350°F (180°C).

Butter and flour two 9 x 5-inch (2 L) loaf pans.

Into a large bowl, sift the flour, cloves, cinnamon, nutmeg, baking soda, baking powder and salt.

Beat the sugar and oil in a separate large bowl until blended. Mix in the eggs and pumpkin.

Stir the flour mix into the pumpkin mixture in 2 additions. Mix in the pecans or walnuts, if using.

Divide the batter equally between the prepared pans. Bake until a wooden pick inserted into the centre of the cake comes out clean, about 1 hour and 10 minutes. Transfer to a cooling rack and cool for 10 minutes.

Use a sharp knife to cut around the edge of the loaves. Turn the loaves out onto racks and cool completely.

Variation: Instead of nuts, add chocolate chips.

3 cups (750 mL) all-purpose flour

½ teaspoon (2 mL) ground cloves

1 teaspoon (5 mL) cinnamon

½ teaspoon (2 mL) ground nutmeg

1 teaspoon (5 mL) baking soda

½ teaspoon (2 mL) baking powder

½ teaspoon (2 mL) salt

2¾ cups (675 mL) sugar

⅔ cup (150 mL) vegetable oil

3 large eggs

2 cups (500 mL) solid packed pumpkin

1 cup (250 mL) coarsely chopped toasted pecans or walnuts, optional

Rebetzin's Coffee Cake

MAKES: 1 BUNDT CAKE

An irresistible cake that is moist and addictive! For variety and colour, add handfuls of dried cranberries, dried cherries, dried apricots and toasted pecans to the cinnamon/sugar mixture. Streusal comes from the German word streuen, *which means to sprinkle or to scatter.*

STREUSEL

½ cup (125 mL) packed brown sugar

1 teaspoon (5 mL) cinnamon

1 cup (250 mL) miniature chocolate chips, optional

½ cup (125 mL) chopped toasted pecans, optional

BATTER

½ cup (125 mL) unsalted butter, at room temperature

1 cup (250 mL) sugar

2 large eggs, at room temperature

1 teaspoon (5 mL) vanilla extract

1 cup (250 mL) sour cream or plain yogurt

2 cups (500 mL) all-purpose flour

1 teaspoon (5 mL) baking powder

1 teaspoon (5 mL) baking soda

Preheat oven to 350°F (180°C).

Grease a 10-cup (2.5 L) Bundt pan.

For the streusel, combine the brown sugar, cinnamon, chocolate chips, if using, and pecans, if using, in a small bowl.

For the batter, in a large mixing bowl, cream together the butter and sugar until fluffy. Add the eggs, one at a time, and blend. Add the vanilla and sour cream or yogurt and mix well.

In a separate bowl, combine the flour, baking powder and baking soda. Gently mix the dry ingredients into the liquid ingredients. Do not overmix.

Pour half the batter into the bottom of the Bundt pan. Sprinkle half the streusel mixture over the batter. Top with the remaining batter and then with the streusel. Bake for 40–45 minutes or until set. Cool on rack.

Variation: To preserve the feeling of summer, add 1 cup (250 mL) blueberries along with the streusel mixture in the centre of the cake.

Chef's tip | EGGS SHOULD BE CRACKED INTO A GLASS BOWL ONE AT A TIME SO THAT YOU CAN SPOT PIECES OF EGGSHELL.

Harvest Bran Muffins

Ⓕ Ⓓ

MAKES: 12 MUFFINS

A healthy muffin free of cholesterol and packed with flavour and texture from the variety of dried fruit. The secret to light muffins is to not overmix the batter or you will end up with golfballs!

Preheat oven to 400°F (200°C). Lightly grease a muffin pan.

In a large bowl, mix together the bran, flour, sugar, cinnamon, baking powder, baking soda and salt. Remove any lumps of sugar.

In another bowl, combine the oil and buttermilk.

Gently mix the wet ingredients into the dry and stir just until combined. The batter will be lumpy. Add the dried fruit and nuts.

Divide the dough to fill 12 muffin cups, half full. Bake for 14–16 minutes until firm. Remove from oven and cool on rack.

Variations: Use half whole wheat flour and half all-purpose to add more fibre. Using all whole wheat flour would make the muffins too heavy.
♦ Replace bran with rolled oats.

Chef's tips | BUTTERMILK IS LOW-FAT MILK THAT IS SLIGHTLY THICK AND IS TANGY IN FLAVOUR. (SEE PANTRY NOTES ON PAGE 17 FOR INSTRUCTIONS ON HOW TO MAKE YOUR OWN BUTTERMILK.)

PAPER MUFFIN CUP LINERS HELP MAKE CLEANUP EASIER AND ALSO HELP TO KEEP MUFFINS MOIST AND PREVENT THEM FROM DRYING OUT.

---

1 cup (250 mL) whole bran
1 cup (250 mL) all-purpose flour
¾ cup (185 mL) packed brown sugar
1 teaspoon (5 mL) cinnamon
1 teaspoon (5 mL) baking powder
½ teaspoon (2 mL) baking soda
pinch of salt
½ cup (125 mL) canola oil
1 cup (250 mL) buttermilk
½ cup (125 mL) raisins or dried cranberries
¼ cup (60 mL) chopped apricots
¼ cup (60 mL) chopped pecans

Cinnamon Sticky Buns

MAKES: 12 BUNS

Nothing is more appreciated than a fresh homemade sticky bun with a hot cup of coffee. These can be prepared in advance and frozen.

Dough

1 packet (2½ teaspoons / 12 mL) rapid yeast or bread machine yeast

3 cups (750 mL) unbleached all-purpose flour

⅓ cup (75 mL) sugar

½ teaspoon (2 mL) salt

½ cup /125 mL unsalted butter or margarine, cut into chunks

2 large eggs

⅓ cup (75 mL) warm milk

¼ cup (60 mL) warm water

1 tablespoon (15 mL) cinnamon

¾ cup (185 mL) packed brown sugar

½ cup (125 mL) raisins, optional

Egg wash

1 egg, beaten

½ teaspoon (2 mL) milk or cream

Fondant icing

1 cup (250 mL) sifted confectioners' sugar

1–2 tablespoons (15–30 mL) milk

For the dough, lightly grease a 9 x 9-inch (2.5 L) metal baking dish with cooking spray.

Bread machine method: Place the dry ingredients in the breadmaker bowl followed by the butter, eggs, milk and water. Select the "dough" cycle. When the cycle is complete, remove the dough from the breadmaker and place in large bowl, loosely covered by a tea towel, to rest for 20 minutes. To test if the dough is ready, poke it with your finger. It should spring back.

Food processor or stand mixer method: In a large Pyrex measuring cup, whisk together the eggs, milk and water. Heat in the microwave for about 30 seconds until warm. Stir.

Place the dry ingredients in the food processor bowl and mix. Add the wet ingredients and the butter. Blend and knead until the dough forms a smooth ball. If it is too sticky, add more flour but try not to add too much because it will make your dough tough. Allow the dough to rest for 20 minutes.

Preheat oven to 350°F (180°C).

Roll the dough into an 18 x 12-inch (45 x 30-cm) rectangle on a lightly floured surface. Sprinkle with the cinnamon, brown sugar and raisins, if using. Roll the dough away from you into a long cylinder. Pinch the seam tightly to keep it closed. Slice into twelve 2-inch (5-cm) pieces. Set the pieces in the baking dish on their side so you can see the swirl of cinnamon, and press down slightly.

For the egg wash, whisk together the beaten egg and milk or cream. Brush it over the dough to give the rolls a golden hue.

Bake the rolls for 20–25 minutes or until golden. Cool them on a wire rack to prevent them from getting soggy.

For the fondant icing, whisk together the sugar and milk. Adjust the consistency until the icing coats the back of a spoon. Drizzle over the buns while they are still warm.

Chef's tips | RAPID YEAST IS THE SAME AS BREAD MACHINE YEAST. THEY BOTH CONTAIN ASCORBIC ACID.

A TOO-COOL LIQUID WILL SLOW OR STOP THE YEAST ACTION. A TOO-HOT LIQUID WILL DESTROY THE YEAST AND PREVENT IT FROM RISING.

Spanakopita

ⒻⒹ

SERVES: 10–12

𝒯he lightness and versatility of Greek "phyllo" (meaning leaf) dough can be enjoyed with a multitude of fillings. This spinach and feta combination can also be wrapped in triangles for bite-size enjoyment. Allow phyllo dough to thaw overnight at room temperature.

2 tablespoons (30 mL) olive oil

1 large onion, cut into small dice

1 leek, white and light green parts, cleaned well and chopped

2 green onions, both green and white parts, chopped

3 tablespoons (45 mL) white wine

3 10-ounce (300-g) bags fresh spinach, cleaned and spun dry

1 bunch Swiss chard, large ribs removed, cleaned and dried

2 large eggs

1 cup (250 mL) chopped packed fresh dill

½ pound (250 g) feta cheese, crumbled

¼ teaspoon (1 mL) kosher salt

¼ teaspoon (1 mL) freshly ground pepper

¼ cup (60 mL) melted unsalted butter or olive oil

8 sheets frozen phyllo pastry (14 x 18 inches / 35 x 45 cm), thawed

sesame seeds

Heat the oil over medium-high heat in a 6-quart (6 L) stockpot. Sauté the onion, leek and green onions until the onions are translucent and the leek is soft.

Add the wine and cook until the alcohol evaporates, about 4 minutes. Add the spinach and Swiss chard; cover and cook until wilted, stirring occasionally, for about 5 minutes. Remove the lid and cook until the vegetables are very soft. Drain thoroughly and discard the liquid. Cool.

Beat the eggs and combine with the dill and feta cheese. Mix with the cooled greens. Add salt and pepper to taste.

Brush the bottom of a 9 x 13-inch (3.5 L) baking dish with melted butter or oil. Cut the phyllo sheets in half to fit the pan. Cover the phyllo with 2 overlapping sheets of plastic wrap and then a dampened kitchen towel to prevent it from drying out. Lay 1 cut sheet of phyllo on the bottom of the pan and brush evenly with melted butter or oil. Repeat the layering and buttering 7 more times, brushing each sheet lightly with melted butter or oil before laying the next sheet on top.

Spread the spinach and feta filling evenly over the layers of phyllo pastry. Cover the filling with 8 more sheets of phyllo, brushing each sheet lightly with melted butter or oil. Brush the top layer with butter or oil and sprinkle with sesame seeds.

Bake at 350°F (180°C) degrees for about 35 minutes or until golden brown. Cut into squares and serve.

Variation: For a dairy-free version, substitute crumbled tofu for the feta. Adjust the seasonings.

Freezing: The filling can be prepared ahead of time and frozen for 1 month. Unbaked spanakopita can be frozen and baked from frozen, uncovered, at 350°F (180°C) for 1 hour.

Frittata with Feta, Sun-Dried Tomatoes and Basil

SERVES: 4–6

A versatile Italian oven-baked omelet. Be sure to use an ovenproof skillet.

Preheat broiler. Arrange baking rack at least 6 inches away from broiler.

Whisk the eggs and milk together in a large bowl. Stir in the feta, sun-dried tomatoes, green onions, basil, salt and pepper.

Melt the butter in a large ovenproof nonstick skillet over medium-high heat. Add the egg mixture but do not stir. Continue to cook on medium-high heat until the eggs start to firm and the sides and bottom begin to brown, lifting the sides occasionally to allow uncooked egg to run underneath, about 5 minutes.

Sprinkle with olives and Parmesan cheese. Transfer the skillet to the oven and cook until the eggs start to puff and brown, about 2 minutes. Watch carefully to avoid burning. Remove from the oven. Using a flexible spatula, loosen the edges and bottom of the frittata and slide onto a plate. Slice the frittata into wedges. Garnish with the parsley. Serve warm or at room temperature.

Variation: For a Sunday morning twist, combine roasted potatoes, smoked salmon and fresh dill in a frittata.

10 large eggs

¼ cup (60 mL) milk

1½ cups (375 mL) crumbled feta cheese (about 6 ounces / 175 g)

10 oil-packed sun-dried tomatoes, drained and finely chopped

4 green onions, both green and white parts, thinly sliced

⅓ cup (75 mL) finely chopped fresh basil leaves

½ teaspoon (2 mL) kosher salt

¼ teaspoon (1 mL) freshly ground pepper

¼ cup (60 mL) unsalted butter

⅓ cup (75 mL) kalamata olives, pitted and thinly sliced

3 tablespoons (45 mL) freshly grated Parmesan cheese

chopped fresh flat-leaf parsley or basil, for garnish

Chef's tip | ALWAYS STORE EGGS IN THEIR CARTON BECAUSE THEY ARE POROUS AND WILL ABSORB THE ODOURS OF YOUR REFRIGERATOR.

Herring Salad with Fresh Dill

SERVES: 4–6

A colourful dish that always gets rave reviews. Serve in a bowl lined with radicchio and curly lettuce.

1 16-ounce (500-g) jar herring pieces in wine sauce

1 cup (250 mL) sour cream

½ cup (125 mL) thinly sliced red onion

1 tomato, diced

½ cucumber, peeled, seeded and diced

½ red bell pepper, diced

2–4 tablespoons (30–60 mL) fresh chopped dill

freshly ground pepper

fresh chopped chives, for garnish

Drain the herring well and cut into bite-size pieces. Add the sour cream, onion, tomato, cucumber, bell pepper and dill, and refrigerate for at least 4 hours, or overnight, before serving.

Season with pepper to taste and garnish with chopped chives.

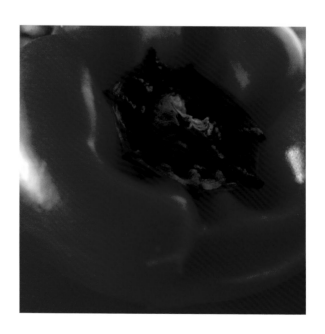

White Fish Salad

Ⓟ

SERVES: 6–8

A light version of a traditional brunch staple. Poaching fish is a quick cooking method that requires little skill and adds great moisture and flavour without any added fat. This salad can be dressed up to 2 hours in advance. You can poach the fish 1 day ahead and wrap in plastic wrap.

For the poaching liquid, bring the wine and water to a boil in a large shallow pan, uncovered, over high heat. Stir in the lemon, peppercorns, bay leaf and celery tops. Reduce the heat and simmer for 5 minutes.

For the fish, gently place the fish in the poaching liquid. Cover the pan and adjust the heat so the liquid is simmering gently. Cook for about 7 minutes then check for doneness. The fish should be opaque inside and should flake with a fork.

Remove the fish. Cool and flake with a fork.

In a large bowl, combine the fish, celery, onions and cucumber.

For the dressing, combine the dressing ingredients and pour over the salad. Toss gently and season to taste.

Variation: Smoked white fish may be used instead of poached fish.

Chef's tip | SEEDING A CUCUMBER: CUT THE CUCUMBER IN HALF LENGTHWISE. USE A SPOON TO SCRAPE OUT THE SEEDS FOR A TUNNEL EFFECT.

POACHING LIQUID
1 cup (250 mL) white wine

1 cup (250 mL) water

½ lemon, sliced

5 peppercorns

1 bay leaf

3–4 celery tops

FISH
3 pounds (1.5 kg) meaty white fish fillets (to make 3–4 cups / 750 mL–1 L flaked fish)

½ cup (125 mL) finely chopped celery

½ cup (125 mL) finely chopped onions or green onions, both white and green parts

1 large cucumber, peeled, seeded and chopped

DRESSING
1 tablespoon (15 mL) chopped fresh tarragon

2 tablespoon (30 mL) chopped fresh flat-leaf parsley

¼ cup (60 mL) fresh lemon juice

1 teaspoon (5 mL) kosher salt

¾ teaspoon (4 mL) freshly ground pepper

1 cup (250 mL) olive oil

Pickled Salmon

SERVES: 6

A traditional favourite that must be prepared in advance. A nice addition to any holiday buffet.

2 cups (500 mL) water

1 cup (250 mL) vinegar

1 cup (250 mL) sugar

2 bay leaves

3 whole cloves

10 peppercorns

1 teaspoon (5 mL) kosher salt

3 onions, sliced

2 pounds (1 kg) salmon fillets cut into 1-inch (2.5-cm) pieces

purple kale

In a saucepan, blend the water, vinegar, sugar, bay leaves, cloves, peppercorns, salt and onions. Bring to a boil. Add the fish and simmer gently for 5 minutes.

Transfer everything to a glass bowl. Once cooled, cover and refrigerate for 3 days. Fish will keep refrigerated for up to 2 weeks. Remove the bay leaves, and serve cold.

To serve, line a platter with purple kale to contrast with the salmon.

Montreal Big Orange Whipped Smoothie

Ⓟ

MAKES: 4 CUPS (1 L)

A Montreal favourite, the Big Orange has been part of our cultural—and visual—landscape for many years. Though you probably will not drink it in your car, this version is just as good as the real thing—maybe even better!

Combine the juice, water, egg whites or egg substitute, vanilla and sugar in a blender. Blend at high speed for 15–30 seconds until the sugar dissolves.

Add the ice. Blend for a further 10–15 seconds until the ice is mostly crushed but still a bit coarse.

Pour into a tall glass and enjoy!

1½ cups (375 mL) orange juice

½ cup (125 mL) water

3 tablespoons (45 mL) egg whites or egg substitute, optional

1 teaspoon (5 mL) vanilla extract

¼ cup (60 mL) sugar

1½ cups (375 mL) ice

❦

Previous page: Roast Chicken Provençal

Chicken Breasts
with Cranberries and Pine Nuts

Ⓕ Ⓜ

SERVES: 4

A colourful festive dish with an interesting combination of textures and flavours. Be sure to choose chicken breasts that are all about the same size to guarantee uniform cooking. Serve with Israeli couscous and spinach.

In a large skillet, heat 2 teaspoons (10 mL) of the olive oil over medium heat. Add the green onions and pine nuts and stir for 1 minute. Add the cranberries, honey, and oregano. Cook for 1 more minute, until the cranberries are softened. Remove from the heat and cool.

Lightly pound the chicken breasts between 2 sheets of plastic wrap to flatten them slightly. Arrange them in a single layer on a plate and freeze for about 15 minutes to make them easier to slice.

Use a sharp knife to slice each breast horizontally, almost in half, along one edge to open like a book (this technique is called *butterflying*). Open each breast up and season with salt and pepper. Divide the cranberry mixture into 4 portions and spoon each portion onto 1 half of each breast. Close the breasts, pressing gently to seal.

In a wide shallow bowl, season the flour with salt and pepper. Dredge the breasts lightly in the flour mixture, shaking off any excess. Set on a platter. The chicken can be prepared up to this point and refrigerated for up to 24 hours before cooking.

Heat the remaining oil in a skillet over medium heat. Once hot, add the chicken, and cook for about 4 minutes, turning once, until lightly browned on each side. Remove and cover with aluminum foil to keep warm.

In the same skillet, combine the stock, vinegar and mustard. Bring to a boil, and reduce the heat to medium low. Add the chicken and cook, covered, for 6–8 minutes or until the chicken is cooked.

To serve, arrange the breasts on dinner plates and drizzle with the cooking juices.

2 tablespoons (30 mL) olive oil

2 green onions, both green and white parts, chopped

3 tablespoons (45 mL) pine nuts, toasted

½ cup (125 mL) cranberries (fresh or frozen)

1 tablespoon (15 mL) honey

1 teaspoon (5 mL) dry oregano

4 large boneless, skinless chicken breasts

½ teaspoon (2 mL) kosher salt plus extra to season flour

3 tablespoons (45 mL) all-purpose flour

freshly ground pepper

½ cup (125 mL) chicken or vegetable stock or ¼ cup (60 mL) stock plus ¼ cup (60 mL) red wine

1 tablespoon (15 mL) balsamic vinegar

1 tablespoon (15 mL) Dijon mustard

Chicken Piccata

SERVES: 4

A tangy and light classic Italian-inspired dish. Serve with Brussels Sprouts with Pecans (see page 172) and Rice with Vermicelli, Green Onions and Garlic (see page 180).

2 pounds (1 kg) boneless, skinless chicken breasts, split in half

3 tablespoons (45 mL) all-purpose flour or matzo meal

½ teaspoon (2 mL) freshly ground pepper

2 tablespoons (30 mL) olive oil

½ cup (125 mL) dry vermouth or white wine

2 tablespoons (30 mL) fresh lemon juice

½ teaspoon (2 mL) kosher salt

1 tablespoon (15 mL) minced fresh thyme or 1 teaspoon (5 mL) dry

1 tablespoon (15 mL) freshly grated lemon zest

Flatten the chicken breasts between two pieces of plastic wrap or in a resealable plastic bag so they are all the same thickness.

Combine the flour and pepper and lightly dredge each breast just before cooking.

Heat the oil in a 12-inch (30-cm) skillet over medium heat. Add the chicken and sauté until lightly golden, about 3 minutes on each side or until done. Transfer to a serving platter and loosely cover with aluminum foil to keep warm.

Slowly add the vermouth or white wine and lemon juice to the skillet to deglaze the pan. Increase the heat to medium and bring the mixture to a boil, scraping up any fragments left in the bottom of the pan with a wooden spoon. Season with salt and more pepper, if desired, and stir in the thyme and lemon zest.

Remove from heat, spoon the sauce over the chicken and serve.

Variations: Use veal scallops instead of chicken. ♦ Vermouth can always be substituted for white wine.

Chef's tip | YOU CAN FREEZE LEFTOVER CITRUS ZEST WRAPPED TIGHTLY IN PLASTIC WRAP. THE GRATED ZEST OF CITRUS FRUITS ADDS GREAT FLAVOUR TO BAKING AND COOKING. MAKE SURE TO AVOID INCLUDING ANY BITTER WHITE PITH.

Chicken Baked
with Artichoke Hearts

Ⓜ

SERVES: 4–6

This simple dish is bursting with flavour and uses common pantry ingredients. A terrific make-ahead dish that stays warm in the oven while you enjoy the company of your guests.

Preheat oven to 350°F (180°C).

Mix the bread crumbs with the paprika, salt and pepper. Dredge the chicken in the crumbs and set aside. Discard remaining crumbs.

Heat the oil in a large skillet on medium-high heat. When hot, place the breasts in the pan to sear. Do not crowd. Sauté for 3 minutes on each side or until browned. Remove the chicken and place in 9 x 13-inch (23 x 32-cm) baking dish.

Wipe out any leftover burned bread crumbs from the skillet and sauté the shallots for 2 minutes. Add more oil if needed. Add the garlic and mushrooms. Make sure the mushrooms are spread out and not on top of each other to ensure a nice searing effect. If the pan gets dry, sprinkle with a drop of wine.

Pour the mushroom mixture, the artichoke hearts, green onions, capers, chicken stock and wine over the chicken. Bake uncovered for about 25 minutes or until cooked through.

Right before serving, squeeze the lemon juice over the chicken as soon as it has been removed from the oven and sprinkle with the chopped parsley to garnish.

Chef's tip | CHICKEN IS PROPERLY COOKED IF THE JUICES RUN CLEAR AND THERE IS NO PINK HUE WHEN THE CHICKEN IS PRICKED WITH A FORK.

1 cup (250 mL) unseasoned bread crumbs or matzo meal

1 teaspoon (5 mL) paprika

1 teaspoon (5 mL) kosher salt

freshly ground pepper

2 pounds (1 kg) boneless, skinless chicken breasts, split in half

¼ cup (60 mL) olive oil

2 dry shallots, minced

2 cloves garlic, minced

1 cup (250 mL) sliced button mushrooms

1 14-ounce (398-mL) can artichoke hearts, drained and halved

2 green onions, both green and white parts, chopped

1 tablespoon (15 mL) drained capers

½ cup (125 mL) chicken stock

1 cup (250 mL) white wine

juice of ½ lemon

fresh chopped flat-leaf parsley, for garnish

Balsamic Glazed Chicken with Mushrooms

SERVES: 4

The dark, sweet Italian balsamic vinegar is aged in barrels made from various types of wood over long periods of time.

3 tablespoons (45 mL) balsamic vinegar

2 teaspoons (10 mL) Dijon mustard

1 large clove garlic, crushed

2 pounds (1 kg) boneless, skinless chicken breasts, about 4 pieces

2 teaspoons (10 mL) olive oil

2 cups (500 mL) cremini mushrooms or wild mushrooms, halved

⅓ cup (75 mL) chicken stock

¼ teaspoon (1 mL) dry thyme, crumbled

In a medium-size bowl, mix 2 tablespoons (30 mL) of the vinegar with the mustard and garlic. Add the chicken and turn it to coat well. Marinate for 1 hour in the refrigerator.

Heat 1 teaspoon (5 mL) of the oil in a nonstick skillet on medium-high heat. Transfer the chicken and marinade to the skillet. Sauté the chicken until cooked through, about 5 minutes per side. Transfer to a platter and loosely cover with aluminum foil to keep warm.

Heat the remaining teaspoon (5 mL) of oil in a skillet and sauté the mushrooms until golden. Add the stock, thyme and remaining vinegar. Return the chicken to the skillet to warm through, about 3 minutes.

Serve the chicken topped with the mushrooms.

Variation: Try using dry white wine instead of the chicken stock, and add a few spoonfuls of chopped sun-dried tomatoes with the mushrooms.

Chef's tips | NEVER SOAK MUSHROOMS IN WATER TO CLEAN THEM. EITHER BRUSH THEM WITH A DAMP PAPER TOWEL OR, IF YOU HAVE A LARGE AMOUNT, PLUNGE THEM IN COLD WATER AND DRAIN IMMEDIATELY IN A COLANDER. GENTLY TOWEL DRY.

CHOOSING THE RIGHT SIZE COOKING PAN IS VITAL. COOKING IN A PAN THAT ENABLES FOODS TO BE "COMFORTABLY CROWDED" HELPS KEEP THEM MOIST. TOO LARGE A PAN WILL DRY THE CHICKEN OUT, WHILE TOO SMALL A PAN WILL NOT ENABLE THE CHICKEN TO COOK EVENLY.

Lemon Herb
Marinated Grilled Chicken

Serves: 4

A quick marinade with a Mediterannean twist. Always spray your grill with nonstick spray before heating to prevent food from sticking. The chicken may also be broiled.

Mix together the olive oil, garlic, vinegar, oregano, lemon zest, lemon juice, pepper and salt. Add the chicken to the marinade and keep for up to 12 hours in the refrigerator.

Preheat grill pan. Spray pan with nonstick spray. Grill chicken for 2–3 minutes per side. Baste frequently and place in a warm 350°F (180°C) oven to finish cooking.

If grilling outside, preheat the grill to medium-high heat and set the grill rack about 4 inches (10 cm) away from the heat source. Grill for 6–7 minutes per side. If cooking chicken on the bone, you will need to increase the cooking time. Grill the chicken until the juices run clear.

Variation: Use the marinade on fish or vegetables for a zesty treat.

Chef's tip | MARINATING IN A RESEALABLE PLASTIC BAG ALLOWS BETTER ABSORPTION AND TAKES UP LESS SPACE IN YOUR REFRIGERATOR.

¼ cup (60 mL) olive oil

5 cloves garlic, crushed

2 tablespoons (30 mL) white wine vinegar

2½ teaspoons (20 mL) dry oregano

1 teaspoon (5 mL) freshly grated lemon zest, about 1 lemon

2½ tablespoons (37 mL) fresh lemon juice

½ teaspoon (2 mL) freshly ground pepper

½ teaspoon (2 mL) kosher salt

4 chicken breasts, boneless or on the bone

Santa Fe Cornmeal-Crusted Chicken
with Toasted Corn Salsa

SERVES: 4

A southwestern-inspired dish. The salsa adds an array of colour and zesty blend of flavours. Beets tend to bleed, so prepare the salsa no more than 1 hour before serving.

TOASTED CORN SALSA

3 tablespoons (45 mL) extra-virgin olive oil

2 cups (500 mL) fresh corn kernels, cut from about 4 ears

2 tablespoons (30 mL) fresh lime juice (about 1 lime)

1 garlic clove, minced and mashed to a paste with a pinch of salt

kosher salt

freshly ground pepper

¼ cup (60 mL) packed cilantro sprigs, washed, spun dry and chopped finely

1 cup (250 mL) diced peeled mango

1 cup (250 mL) drained bottled pickled beets, diced

¼ cup (60 mL) finely chopped green onions, both green and white parts

CHICKEN

4 skinless boneless chicken breasts

kosher salt

freshly ground pepper

½ cup (125 mL) yellow cornmeal

½ teaspoon (2 mL) paprika

½ teaspoon (2 mL) cayenne pepper

1–2 tablespoons (15–30 mL) olive oil

For the salsa, heat 1 tablespoon (15 mL) of the oil over moderately high heat in a nonstick skillet until hot but not smoking. Sauté the corn, stirring until deep golden, about 4 minutes.

In a medium-size bowl, whisk together 2 tablespoons (30 mL) of the oil, the lime juice, garlic paste, salt and pepper. Add the corn, cilantro, mango, beets and green onions and toss to combine well. Set aside.

Pat the chicken dry and season with salt and pepper.

In a shallow baking dish, stir together the cornmeal, paprika and cayenne and press the chicken into the mixture, coating both sides. Let stand for 5 minutes and allow coating to set.

In a large nonstick skillet, heat the oil over moderately high heat and sauté the chicken until golden and cooked through, about 5 minutes on each side.

To serve, place chicken on a plate and top with a scoop of salsa.

Chef's tip | WHEN HANDLING RAW CHICKEN, USE A SEPARATE CUTTING BOARD AND MAKE SURE TO WASH HANDS AND UTENSILS IN WARM SOAPY WATER TO PREVENT CROSS-CONTAMINATION.

Roast Chicken with Fresh Tarragon and Garlic

SERVES: 8

A *simple succulent dish. Tarragon is an herb with an anise flavour that is often associated with French cuisine.*

Preheat oven to 400°F (200°C).

Mix together the margarine and tarragon.

Place the chicken breasts in 9 x 13-inch (3.5-L) roasting pan.

Rub the chicken with the margarine mixture. Season lightly with salt and pepper.

Scatter garlic cloves around the chicken breasts and roast uncovered for about 1 hour, basting every 20 minutes. Remove from oven and set aside the garlic cloves.

Remove the chicken from the pan, place it on a serving platter and cover loosely with aluminum foil. Let rest for 10 minutes.

Remove 2 tablespoons (30 mL) of the fat from the roasting pan and place in a skillet. Set aside for the gravy.

To deglaze the roasting pan, pour in the stock and bring to a boil, scraping up the bits from the bottom of the pan. Add the garlic cloves and any accumulated juices from the chicken.

Reheat the fat over medium heat, sprinkle in the flour or matzo cake meal and stir until the flour turns golden brown, about 1 minute. Add the stock to the roux and simmer 3–5 minutes, stirring, until the stock has thickened.

Sprinkle in the fresh tarragon. Season with salt and pepper. Simmer until the flavours intensify, about 3–5 minutes.

Pour the gravy over the chicken, scatter garlic cloves over the platter, and serve.

2 tablespoons (30 mL) unsalted margarine, at room temperature

2 tablespoons (30 mL) chopped fresh tarragon or 2 teaspoons (10 mL) dry

4 pounds (2 kg) chicken breasts with bone and skin intact

kosher salt

freshly ground pepper

8 cloves garlic

1 tablespoons (15 mL) all-purpose flour or matzo cake meal

1½ cups (375 mL) chicken stock

1 teaspoon (5 mL) fresh tarragon

Chef's tip | 1 TEASPOON (5 mL) OF DRY HERB IS EQUIVALENT TO 1 TABLESPOON (15 mL) OF FRESH HERB.

Chicken Provençal

SERVES: 4

*M*editerranean baked chicken with tomatoes, potatoes and olives. Truly a one-dish wonder. Garnish with chopped fresh flat-leaf parsley to add colour.

14 cloves garlic

1 teaspoon (5 mL) kosher salt

2 tablespoons (30 mL) fresh lemon juice

¼ cup (60 mL) olive oil

2 large lemons, thinly sliced

4 chicken breasts, with skin and bone

kosher salt

freshly ground pepper

2 pounds (1 kg) small red potatoes, quartered

8 plum (Roma) tomatoes, halved lengthwise

2 tablespoons (30 mL) fresh rosemary or 2 teaspoons (10 mL) dry rosemary

20 kalamata olives, pitted and sliced

Preheat oven to 450°F (230°C).

Oil a 9 x 13-inch (3.5 L) shallow baking pan.

Mince and mash 2 of the garlic cloves to a paste with the salt. In a small bowl, whisk together the garlic paste, lemon juice and 2 tablespoons (30 mL) of the oil.

In the prepared pan, make 4 separate beds of overlapping lemon slices and put a chicken breast on each bed. Brush the chicken with half of the lemon and garlic mixture and season with salt and pepper.

Toss the potatoes, tomatoes, remaining garlic cloves, rosemary and the remaining oil together and coat well. Place around the chicken.

Roast uncovered in the middle of the oven for 20 minutes. Remove from the oven and brush with the remaining lemon and garlic mixture. Add the olives and roast 20–25 minutes more or until the chicken is thoroughly cooked and the juices run clear.

Discard the lemon slices and serve the chicken with the vegetables and pan juices spooned over.

Variation: Substitute a whole chicken cut into pieces for the breasts.

Chef's tip | TO PIT AN OLIVE, PLACE IT ON A CUTTING BOARD. WITH THE FLAT SIDE OF A FRENCH KNIFE BANG THE OLIVE AND "BRUISE" IT TO LOOSEN THE FLESH FROM THE PIT. REMOVE THE PIT.

Caribbean Chicken

SERVES: 4

A delicious dish reminscent of the tropical islands. The combination of allspice and green onions gives an authentic West Indies aroma to this dish.

Season the chicken with salt and pepper

Heat the oil in a large skillet on medium-high heat.

Add the chicken to the skillet, skin side down, and brown for 5 minutes. Turn the chicken over and brown for 3 minutes longer. Remove from the skillet.

Drain off the pan juices, leaving about 1 tablespoon (15 mL) in the skillet and reduce the heat to medium. Add the ginger, garlic and green onion to the skillet. Sauté for about 1 minute. Add the cumin and allspice and sauté for about 30 seconds, until you can smell the spices. Add the lime juice, rum, chicken stock and orange juice. Bring to a boil.

Return the chicken to the skillet, reduce the heat to medium-low, cover and cook for about 20 minutes or until the chicken juices run clear. Remove the chicken to a plate, and cover loosely with aluminum foil to keep warm. Add the cilantro and parsley to the sauce in the skillet, and bring to a boil. Reduce the sauce over high heat for about 2 minutes or until slightly thickened.

Pour the sauce over the chicken and garnish with cashews.

Variation: Dark or golden rum can be used instead of white.

Chef's tip | DRY HERBS AND SPICES TEND TO LOSE THEIR STRENGTH OVER TIME, SO REPLACE THEM EVERY 6 MONTHS FOR MORE AROMATIC COOKING AND BAKING. STORE THEM IN YOUR FREEZER TO EXTEND THEIR SHELF LIFE.

1 3-pound (1.5-kg) chicken, cut into 8 pieces

kosher salt

freshly ground pepper

1 tablespoon (15 mL) vegetable oil

1 tablespoon (15 mL) freshly grated ginger

1 teaspoon (5 mL) chopped garlic

1 cup (250 mL) thinly sliced green onion, both green and white parts

2 teaspoons (10 mL) cumin

1 teaspoon (5 mL) allspice

2 tablespoons (30 mL) fresh lime juice

¼ cup (60 mL) white rum

½ cup (125 mL) chicken stock

½ cup (125 mL) orange juice

2 tablespoons (30 mL) chopped fresh cilantro

2 tablespoons (30 mL) chopped fresh flat-leaf parsley

½ cup (125 mL) toasted cashews (see Chef's tip on page 153)

(M)

Moroccan Chicken
with Olives and Preserved Lemons

SERVES: 4

Chicken with lemon and olives is one of the great combinations in Moroccan cooking. Preserved lemons have a unique pickled taste and special silken texture that cannot be duplicated by fresh lemon juice. Serve with couscous for a final touch of authenticity.

4 pounds (2 kg) chicken pieces, both dark and white

1 medium onion, thinly sliced

1 tablespoon (15 mL) grated fresh ginger

½ cup (125 mL) cracked green olives in brine, rinsed and pitted

¼ teaspoon (1 mL) turmeric

pinch of saffron

1 cup (250 mL) water

1 preserved lemon, skin only, rinsed and finely chopped (see recipe on page 115)

2 tablespoons (30 mL) chopped fresh flat-leaf parsley

1½ tablespoons (22 mL) chopped fresh cilantro

freshly ground pepper

Place the chicken, onion, ginger, olives, turmeric, saffron and water in a heavy soup pot and bring to a boil. Reduce the heat to medium-high and cook, covered, for 1 hour.

Add the lemon skin, parsley, cilantro and pepper to taste, and cook for another 10 minutes. Using a slotted spoon, transfer the chicken to a platter.

Cook the sauce over high heat until it is reduced and the flavours intensify, about 10 minutes. Pour over the chicken and serve.

Preserved Lemons

Ⓟ

MAKES: 5 LEMONS

The lemons must be completely covered in salted lemon juice. They will keep for 6 months in the refrigerator. Preserved lemons can also be purchased in specialty food shops.

Rinse the lemons under warm water and score 4 lengthwise slits from top to bottom in each lemon. Rub salt generously into the slits then put the lemons into a sterilized jar. Pack them tightly.

Add fresh lemon juice to within ½ inch (1 cm) from the top of the jar. Cover tightly with a lid and place in a cool dark spot or the refrigerator to cure for 3 weeks. If you see white film developing, just rinse it off.

> 5 lemons, or enough to fill a jar plus extra for juicing
>
> ¼ cup (60 mL) kosher salt

Chicken Chasseur

SERVES: 4

*O*therwise known as Hunter's Chicken, this is a classic French dish that improves over time. Serve family style on a beautiful ceramic dish with a side dish of wide egg noodles.

8 skinless chicken thighs or 1 chicken cut up (3½–4½ pounds / 1.75–2.25 kg), rinsed and patted dry with paper towels

kosher salt

freshly ground pepper

1 tablespoon (15 mL) olive oil

1 small leek, white and light green part, chopped

1 medium onion (1 cup / 250 mL), diced

1 pound (500 g) button mushrooms, sliced

1 tablespoon (15 mL) finely chopped garlic

1 tablespoon (15 mL) all-purpose flour

1 cup (250 mL) dry white wine or vermouth

1 19-ounce (540-mL) can peeled tomatoes

1 tablespoon (15 mL) soy sauce

1 teaspoon (5 mL) chopped fresh thyme

1 teaspoon (5 mL) chopped fresh rosemary

1–2 tablespoons (15–30 mL) chopped fresh flat-leaf parsley

Preheat oven to 350°F (180°C).

Season chicken with salt and pepper.

Heat the oil in a large nonstick skillet. Lightly brown or sear the chicken until it is golden, about 5 minutes per side. Transfer to a 9 x 13-inch (3.5-L) casserole pan in a single layer.

To the same skillet, add the leek and onion and sauté for 1 minute. You may need to add more oil. Add the mushrooms and garlic and cook until the water has evaporated from the mushrooms. Sprinkle the flour over the vegetables and stir for 1 minute. Add the wine or vermouth, tomatoes, soy sauce, thyme and rosemary and simmer for 10 minutes uncovered to thicken and for flavours to meld.

Pour sauce over chicken and bake for 45 minutes to 1 hour.

Garnish with chopped parsley.

Chef's tip | ALWAYS PREHEAT YOUR OVEN TO THE REQUIRED TEMPERATURE TO ENSURE EVEN COOKING.

Sticky Chicken Wings

Ⓜ

SERVES: 10–12

A real crowd pleaser—especially for children. Prepare wings in a disposable aluminum foil roasting pan to make cleanup easier.

Preheat oven to 425°F (220°C).

Cut off the wing tips and halve the wings at the joints. You may prefer to have the butcher do this part. Divide the wings between 2 large roasting pans, arranging them in a single layer.

Mix the lime juice, apricot preserves or jam, soy sauce, sugar and garlic in a bowl and pour over the wings, dividing evenly between the two pans.

Roast in the upper and lower thirds of the oven for 50 minutes. Turn the wings over and switch the positions of the pans in the oven. Bake until the sauce is thick and sticky, about 45 minutes to an hour

Serve warm or at room temperature.

8 pounds (3.5 kg) chicken wings

1 cup (250 mL) fresh lime juice (about 8–10 limes)

1 cup (250 mL) apricot preserves or apricot jam

1 cup (250 mL) soy sauce

⅔ cup (150 mL) sugar

4 large cloves garlic, minced

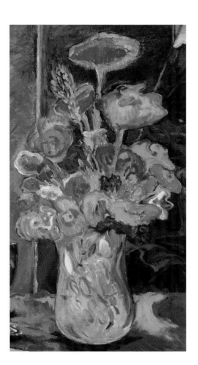

Ⓜ

Chicken Kabobs
with Mango Chutney

Serves: 4

Chutney is a spicy condiment that contains fruit, sugar, vinegar and spices. It can be found in grocery stores or you can easily prepare it yourself. It can be prepared up to 4 days ahead, covered and refrigerated. Warm gently before serving in a small saucepan with 1 tablespoon (15 mL) of water.

⅓ cup (75 mL) hoisin sauce

1 teaspoon (5 mL) toasted sesame oil

3 cloves garlic, minced

1 tablespoon (15 mL) minced fresh ginger

2 tablespoons (30 mL) low-sodium soy sauce

3 tablespoons (45 mL) rice wine vinegar

2 pounds (1 kg) boneless, skinless chicken breasts, cut into 1-inch (2.5-cm) cubes

8 metal skewers or bamboo skewers soaked in water

1 tablespoon (15 mL) sesame seeds, toasted

Combine the hoisin sauce, sesame oil, garlic, ginger, soy sauce and rice vinegar in a medium bowl or plastic bag.

Add the cubed chicken to the marinade. Turn to coat well and refrigerate for at least 1 hour or overnight.

Preheat oven to 400°F (200°C). Line a baking sheet with parchment paper.

Skewer chicken pieces closely together, 4 per skewer, and place skewers in a single layer on the baking sheet. Bake until cooked through, about 7 minutes.

Arrange skewers on a platter, sprinkle with sesame seeds and serve warm with Mango Chutney (see page 119).

Chef's tip | THE PREPARED SKEWERED CHICKEN CAN BE ASSEMBLED AHEAD AND FROZEN. THAW IN THE REFRIGERATOR OVERNIGHT AND COOK AS ABOVE.

Mango Chutney

(P)

MAKES: 2 CUPS (500 mL)

Heat oil in a medium saucepan and sauté the onions and peppers over moderately low heat until the onions are soft and just beginning to brown, about 7 minutes. Reduce the heat, add the mangos and half the lime juice and cook, covered, stirring frequently until the fruit begins to release some of its juices and softens slightly, about 3 minutes.

Remove from the heat. Cool slightly before stirring in the cilantro, basil and remaining lime juice to keep the herbs' colour. Serve warm.

½ teaspoon (2 mL) extra-virgin olive oil

½ cup (125 mL) finely chopped Vidalia or Spanish onions

1 teaspoon (5 mL) minced jalapeño peppers

2 ripe medium mangos, peeled and diced (2 cups / 500 mL)

¼ cup (60 mL) fresh lime juice

¼ cup (60 mL) chopped fresh cilantro

1 tablespoon (15 mL) chopped fresh basil

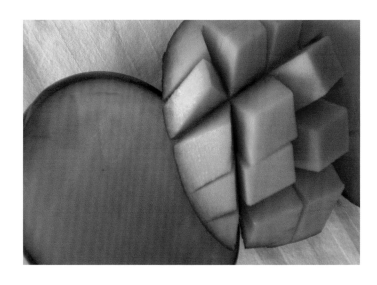

Glazed Honey Mustard Turkey Breast

SERVES: 4

You do not need a special holiday to enjoy turkey. Leftovers make great sandwiches or midnight snacks.

3 cloves garlic, crushed

1–3 tablespoons (15–45 mL) olive oil

3 tablespoons (45 mL) Dijon mustard

6 tablespoons (90 mL) balsamic vinegar or fresh lemon juice

6 tablespoons (90 mL) packed brown sugar or honey

3 tablespoons (45 mL) dry basil

3 tablespoons (45 mL) paprika

freshly ground pepper

2 onions, thinly sliced

½ cup (125 mL) water

1 2–3 pound (1–1.5 kg) turkey breast, bone in and skin on

Preheat oven to 350°F (180°C).

Mix together the garlic, olive oil, Dijon mustard, balsamic vinegar or lemon juice, brown sugar or honey, basil, paprika and pepper in a small bowl.

Spread the onions in a roasting pan. Add the water, then place the turkey breast on top of the onions.

Lift the turkey skin and spoon the garlic mixture underneath.

Roast uncovered for at least 60 minutes, depending on size of breast. Baste frequently.

Let rest for 10 minutes, covered loosely with aluminum foil. Slice and serve.

Chef's tip | LETTING COOKED MEAT REST FOR ABOUT 10 MINUTES BEFORE SLICING IS CRUCIAL TO ALLOW THE JUICES TO PERMEATE THROUGH-OUT. DO NOT WORRY ABOUT THE TURKEY GETTING TOO COLD—IT WILL HOLD THE HEAT.

meat

Previous page: Pan-Seared Steak with Fresh Herb Crust

Pan-Seared Steak
with Fresh Herb Crust

Ⓜ

Serves: 4

Do not be put off by the amount of margarine in this recipe. You only use a small portion of it— the rest can be reserved for other recipes! Serve with mushroom ragout.

For the herb margarine, blend the margarine, bread, basil, parsley, chives, garlic, salt and pepper in a food processor to form a smooth paste.

Using plastic wrap, form the mixture into a cylinder 2 inches (5 cm) in diameter and about 11 inches (28 cm) long. Wrap and refrigerate until needed, or freeze for up to 1 month.

For the mushroom ragout, heat the oil gently in a large skillet. Sauté the shallots for about 4 minutes and add the mushrooms. Cook until the liquid evaporates and the mushrooms are starting to brown.

Add the wine and deglaze the pan. Add the chicken stock and boil until the mixture is reduced by half. Season with salt and pepper and keep warm until needed.

Rub the steaks with oil and season with salt and pepper.

Heat a large heavy skillet over medium heat. Once the pan is hot, sear the steaks on one side for about 5 minutes. Turn over and sear the other side: 3–4 minutes for rare, 5–8 minutes for medium.

To serve, place some mushroom ragout on each of 4 warm plates. Set a steak in the centre of the ragout and garnish with chopped fresh parsley. Place a slice of herb margarine on top of each steak.

Variation: Grill the steaks instead of searing them.

Chef's tips | To roast garlic, slice the top off a bulb of garlic to expose the cloves. Drizzle with a bit of olive oil and wrap in aluminum foil. Roast for 1 hour at 350°F (180°C) or until soft. Cool, then squeeze the cloves out of their thin paper-like peel.

When reducing a liquid mixture, use a chopstick to measure the change in volume.

Herb margarine
½ pound (250 g) margarine, at room temperature

8 slices white bread, crust removed

1 tablespoon (15 mL) chopped fresh basil

1 tablespoon (15 mL) chopped fresh flat-leaf parsley

1 tablespoon (15 mL) chopped fresh chives

5 cloves roasted garlic (see Chef's tip)

kosher salt and freshly ground pepper

Mushroom ragout
1–2 tablespoons (15–30 mL) olive oil

2 tablespoons minced dry shallots

4 cups (1 L) assorted mushrooms (porcini, chanterelles, shiitake, oyster and button), cleaned and cut into quarters

⅓ cup (75 mL) white wine

1 cup (250 mL) chicken stock

kosher salt and freshly ground pepper

Steak
4 5-ounce (150-g) beef steaks (Spencer cut)

1 tablespoon (15 mL) oil

kosher salt and freshly ground pepper

1–2 tablespoons (15–30 mL) chopped fresh parsley

Hoisin London Broil
with Sautéed Mushrooms

SERVES: 4

The longer the steak is marinated, the more tender it becomes. Grilling the meat adds a smokiness that you simply cannot achieve in the oven. The marinade can be prepared up to three days ahead and kept in the refrigerator. Hoisin sauce has a long shelf life and can keep refrigerated indefinitely.

MARINADE

¼ cup (60 mL) soy sauce

¼ cup (60 mL) hoisin sauce

¼ cup (60 mL) rice wine vinegar

2 tablespoons (30 mL) packed brown sugar

2 tablespoons (30 mL) vegetable oil

1 teaspoon (5 mL) minced fresh ginger

1 teaspoon (5 mL) minced garlic

1 1¼-pound (625-g) London broil

MUSHROOMS

1 teaspoon (5 mL) oil

3 cups (750 mL) assorted mushrooms (cremini, portobello, button, oyster), sliced

1 teaspoon (5 mL) minced garlic

¾ cup (185 mL) chopped green onions, both green and white parts

For the marinade, whisk together the soy sauce, hoisin sauce, vinegar, brown sugar, oil, ginger and garlic in a small bowl.

Pour over the steak and marinate in the refrigerator for at least 2 hours or overnight, to a maximum of 2 days. Bring to room temperature before cooking.

Preheat barbecue or broiler.

Barbecue or broil the steak, basting with some of the marinade, until desired doneness, about 3–4 minutes on each side (no more than 10 minutes total). Do not cook beyond medium-rare—it will be tough! Let the meat rest 10 minutes before slicing. Reserve remaining marinade.

For the mushrooms, heat the oil over medium-high heat in a large nonstick skillet. Add the mushrooms. Cook until soft and all the liquid has evaporated, about 7 minutes. Add the garlic and green onions and cook for 1 minute longer.

To make the sauce, bring the remaining marinade to a boil and simmer for 3 minutes. Slice the steak thinly across the grain and serve with sauce and mushrooms.

Chef's tip | YOU KNOW YOUR PAN IS HOT WHEN THE OIL STARTS TO DANCE IN THE PAN.

Stir-Fried Beef
with Ginger and Peppers

SERVES: 4

Stir-frying is a fast cooking method, although preparing stir-fry ingredients can be time-consuming. To save time, purchase pre-cut vegetables. To ensure even cooking, it is essential that everything is cut uniformly. Serve this dish on a bed of rice.

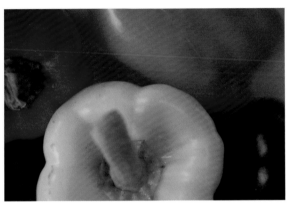

For the marinade, whisk the soy sauce, sherry, sesame oil, sugar and vinegar in a medium bowl. Add the beef, stir to coat and marinate in the refrigerator for 2–4 hours or overnight.

For the stir-fry, heat a large skillet or wok. Add 2 tablespoons (30 mL) of the oil and stir-fry the ginger and garlic over high heat for 1 minute. Add the peppers and onion and stir-fry for about 3 minutes. Season with the salt and pepper and transfer to a bowl. Keep warm.

Heat the remaining oil in the same pan. Add the marinated beef and stir-fry over high heat for 2 to 3 minutes. Return the peppers and onion to the pan. Add the soy sauce and vinegar and stir to combine.

Add the dissolved cornstarch and continue to cook until the sauce begins to thicken.

Transfer to a platter and garnish with toasted sesame seeds. Serve immediately.

Chef's tip | FRESH GINGER IS FIRM AND CRUNCHY. LOOK FOR THE HARDEST, SMOOTHEST-SKINNED GINGER YOU CAN FIND. TO CHECK FOR FRESHNESS, BREAK OFF A PIECE—IT SHOULD SNAP. WRAP ANY LEFTOVER GINGER IN PLASTIC AND STORE IN THE FREEZER FOR LATER USE.

MARINADE

2 tablespoons (30 mL) soy sauce

1 tablespoon (15 mL) dry sherry

4 teaspoons (20 mL) toasted sesame oil

½ teaspoon (2 mL) sugar

1 teaspoon (5 mL) rice wine vinegar

1 pound (500 g) London broil, sliced thinly on the diagonal, against the grain

STIR-FRY

3 tablespoons (45 mL) peanut oil

4 teaspoons (20 mL) peeled and minced fresh ginger

2 medium cloves garlic, sliced

3 bell peppers (1 red, 1 green and 1 yellow), seeded and cut into 1-inch (2.5-cm) slices

1 small red onion, thinly sliced

¼ teaspoon (1 mL) kosher salt

⅛ teaspoon (0.5 mL) freshly ground pepper

1 tablespoon (15 mL) soy sauce

1 teaspoon (5 mL) balsamic vinegar

1 teaspoon (5 mL) cornstarch dissolved in 1 tablespoon (15 mL) water

1–2 tablespoons (15–30 mL) sesame seeds, toasted

Curried Lamb with Apricots

(F)(M)

SERVES: 6

This recipe uses a slow cooker, but an ovenproof covered pot is also an option. Curry is a mixture of different spices that varies from region to region. For a complete comfort meal, serve with couscous or basmati rice.

1 tablespoon (15 mL) vegetable oil

2 pounds (1 kg) stewing lamb, cut into 1-inch (2.5-cm) cubes

2 onions, chopped

4 cloves garlic, minced

1–2 long green chili peppers, chopped

1 teaspoon (5 mL) minced fresh ginger

1 cinnamon stick

1 teaspoon (5 mL) turmeric

1 teaspoon (5 mL) ground coriander

1 teaspoon (5 mL) kosher salt

½ teaspoon (2.5 mL) freshly ground pepper

½ cup (125 mL) beef stock

1½ cups (375 mL) dried apricots

Heat the oil in a large skillet and brown the lamb in batches. Transfer the lamb to a slow cooker.

In the same skillet, cook the onions until soft, about 4 minutes. Add the garlic, peppers, ginger, cinnamon, turmeric, coriander, salt and pepper and cook for 1 minute to bring out the flavours. Add the beef stock and stir.

Pour the mixture over the lamb in the slow cooker, stir in the apricots and cook for 8 to 10 hours on low or 4 to 5 hours on high.

If cooking in a covered pot, cook at 325°F (165°C) for about 1½–2 hours until soft. Cook the lamb beyond the stage of stringiness to the point where the meat is tender and very moist.

Variation: Veal can be used instead of lamb.

Black Pepper and Herb-Crusted Rack of Lamb

SERVES: 4–6

This is an elegant main course dish for a special occasion. Ask your butcher to French-cut the chops by cleaning the fat off the racks and scraping the bones.

Pat the lamb dry with paper towels and brush with oil.

In a small bowl, combine the garlic, pepper, chervil, rosemary, thyme and salt. Rub this into the lamb, then cover and refrigerate for at least 2 hours.

Place a shallow roasting pan in the oven and preheat to 425°F (220°C). Put the lamb racks in the hot pan fat side up and roast for 25 minutes for rare and 30 minutes for medium rare.

Transfer to a cutting board and let stand, covered loosely with aluminum foil, for 10 minutes.

Slice between bones to separate into individual portions, plate and serve.

Chef's tip | LETTING THE MEAT REST FOR A FEW MINUTES ALLOWS THE JUICES TO SET. THIS MAKES CARVING EASIER AND PRODUCES MOIST, FLAVOURFUL MEAT.

4 racks of lamb

1½ tablespoons (20 mL) olive oil

1 clove garlic, minced

1 tablespoon (15 mL) coarsely crushed black pepper

1 tablespoon (15 mL) minced fresh chervil or 1 teaspoon (5 mL) dry chervil

½ tablespoon (7 mL) dry rosemary

¼ teaspoon (1 mL) dry thyme

kosher salt

Ⓕ Ⓜ

Braised Veal Chops
with Gremolata

SERVES: 8

*G*remolata *is a zesty garlic and citrus addition that pairs nicely with the braised veal. Serve with warm egg noodles for a complete dinner.*

VEAL

3 tablespoons (45 mL) olive oil

1½ cups (375 mL) finely chopped onions

½ cup (125 mL) finely chopped carrots

½ cup (125 mL) finely chopped celery

1 clove garlic, finely chopped

8 second cut veal chops

kosher salt

freshly ground pepper

1½ cups (375 mL) all-purpose flour

¼–½ cup (60–125 mL) vegetable
or olive oil

1 cup (250 mL) white wine
or dry vermouth

¾ cup (185 mL) chicken stock

½ teaspoon (2 mL) dry thyme
or oregano

½ teaspoon (2 mL) dry basil

3 tablespoons (45 mL) chopped
fresh flat-leaf parsley

3 cups (750 mL) drained, canned
whole tomatoes, coarsely chopped

12 ounces (375 g) wide egg noodles

GREMOLATA

1 tablespoon (15 mL) grated lemon zest

1 teaspoon (5 mL) finely chopped
garlic

3 tablespoons (45 mL) finely
chopped fresh flat-leaf parsley

For the veal, heat the 3 tablespoons (45 mL) of oil in large skillet. Sauté the onions, carrots, celery and garlic over moderate heat for about 10 minutes. Remove from the heat and transfer to a bowl.

Season the chops with salt and pepper. Dredge in flour and shake off any excess. Let stand for 5 minutes.

Heat ¼ cup (60 mL) of oil in the same skillet used to cook the vegetables. Sear the veal chops for about 3 minutes on each side. Add more oil if required, up to ½ cup (125 mL).

Transfer the browned meat to a pot with a cover and add the vegetables. Remove any excess fat from skillet and deglaze with wine or vermouth. Boil the wine or vermouth until reduced to ½ cup (125 mL). Stir in the chicken stock, thyme, basil, parsley and tomatoes and bring to a boil.

Pour the sauce over the veal. Cover the pot and bring to a boil. Reduce heat and simmer, basting occasionally, for about 2 hours.

For the gremolata, combine the lemon zest, garlic and parsley in a small bowl.

Cook noodles according to the package directions and drain.

To serve, place the veal on a bed of cooked noodles and cover with the sauce and vegetables. Sprinkle with gremolata.

Freezing: Veal and sauce may be frozen together.

Chef's tips | BRAISING IS A WET METHOD OF COOKING WHERE THE MEAT IS FIRST BROWNED IN FAT AND THEN COOKED, TIGHTLY COVERED, IN A SMALL AMOUNT OF LIQUID AT LOW HEAT FOR SEVERAL HOURS TO TENDERIZE.

Brisket

Ⓕ Ⓜ

SERVES: 6–8

A traditional holiday favourite that is an easy made-ahead entrée. A slow-cooked cut of meat that tenderizes over time.

Preheat oven to 325°F (165°C).

Blend the garlic, vinegar or lemon juice, wine, oil, honey, cola, ketchup, salt, pepper and paprika either in a food processor or by hand.

Pour the marinade over the brisket, making sure to cover all surfaces. Marinate 2 hours or overnight in the refrigerator.

Spread the sliced onions on the bottom of a large roasting pan. Place the brisket on top of the onions.

Cover the roasting pan well with aluminum foil, making a tight seal. Cook for 3–4 hours, until the brisket is very tender.

Cool, then refrigerate overnight. This will make it easier to trim off the fat and slice the roast the next day into ½ inch (1 cm) slices.

Freezing: The brisket and sauce can be frozen together.

Chef's tip | TO SAVE SPACE IN YOUR REFRIGERATOR, PLACE MEAT IN A LARGE PLASTIC BAG AND ADD THE MARINADE. THIS METHOD ENSURES THE WHOLE BRISKET IS EVENLY COVERED.

3 cloves garlic, minced

2 tablespoons (30 mL) vinegar or fresh lemon juice

¼ cup (60 mL) red wine

½ cup (125 mL) oil

¼ (60 mL) cup honey

1 can cola

3 tablespoons (45 mL) ketchup

1 tablespoon (15 mL) kosher salt

¼ teaspoon (1 mL) freshly ground pepper

1 teaspoon (5 mL) paprika

5 pounds (2.2 kg) beef brisket

2 cups (500 mL) half-moon sliced onions

Pickled Brisket

F M

SERVES: 8

This is an easy make-ahead recipe that improves over time! It's a wonderful Rosh Hashanah dish infused with sweetness for the New Year. Sliced thinly, this brisket tastes like authentic Montreal smoked meat served warm on rye bread with mustard.

4–5 pound (2–2.2 kg) first cut pickled brisket

¼–½ cup (60–125 mL) packed brown sugar

2 tablespoons (30 mL) honey

Preheat oven to 325°F (160°C).

Place the meat in a large roasting pan and rub with the brown sugar and honey. Cover with aluminum foil and bake for 3 hours or until tender.

Cool and refrigerate. Slice cold, against the grain, the following day in ½-inch (1-cm) slices and reheat in pan juices.

Serve with Spinach Soufflé (see page 169).

Beef Tacos

Ⓕ Ⓜ

SERVES: 4

𝒶 fun family dinner that allows everyone to build their own taco.

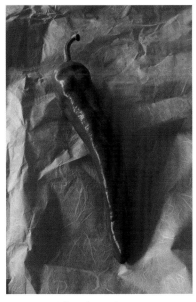

Heat the oil in large nonstick skillet. Add the onion and sauté until translucent, about 5 minutes. Add the garlic, jalapeño pepper, chili powder, cumin, coriander and oregano and stir for 1 minute to bring out flavours. Add the beef and break it down into small pieces with a wooden spoon. Sauté until browned, continuing to break down any remaining lumps.

Add the tomato sauce, chicken stock, brown sugar and vinegar. Cook on medium heat for 10 minutes to reduce but not dry out the sauce. Season with salt and pepper.

Serve in taco shells accompanied by bowls of shredded lettuce, tomatoes, salsa and guacamole.

Freezing: The meat mixture freezes perfectly.

2 teaspoons (10 mL) vegetable oil

1 cup (250 mL) diced onion

2 cloves garlic, minced

1 jalapeño pepper, seeded and minced

2 tablespoons (30 mL) chili powder

1 teaspoon (5 mL) cumin

1 teaspoon (5 mL) coriander

½ teaspoon (2 mL) dry oregano

1 pound (500 g) lean ground beef

½ cup (125 mL) tomato sauce

½ cup (125 mL) chicken stock

1 teaspoon (5 mL) packed brown sugar

2 teaspoons (10 mL) cider vinegar

kosher salt

freshly ground pepper

store-bought taco shells

shredded lettuce

chopped tomatoes

salsa

Guacamole (see page 27)

Sweet and Sour Meatballs

MAKES: 40 MEATBALLS

These meatballs are a big hit with kids. The secret to tender meatballs is gently handling the ground beef and simmering the meatballs for a long time to soften.

SAUCE
1 14-ounce (398-mL) can cranberry sauce

1 28-ounce (796-mL) can diced tomatoes

¼ cup (60 mL) packed brown sugar

1 tablespoon (15 mL) fresh lemon juice

2 tablespoons (30 mL) ketchup

½ teaspoon (2 mL) kosher salt

MEATBALLS
2 cloves garlic, minced

½ cup (125 mL) grated onion, squeezed dry

2 pounds (1 kg) ground beef

1 large egg, beaten

1½ teaspoons (7 mL) kosher salt

freshly ground pepper

For the sauce, pour the cranberry sauce, tomatoes, sugar, lemon juice, ketchup and salt into a large saucepan. Heat slowly and bring to a simmer. Stir frequently to prevent the sauce from burning.

For the meatballs, gently mix the garlic, onion, beef, egg, salt and pepper together in a large mixing bowl. Roll into 40 small uniform balls and drop them gently into the simmering sauce mixture.

Cook, partially covered, at a low simmer for about 2–3 hours, stirring occasionally to prevent burning. Refrigerate overnight and skim off any congealed fat. Best served the day after cooking once flavours have melded together.

Variations: Use chicken or veal in place of the beef and reduce the cooking time. ♦ Use lean ground beef to lower the fat content.

fish

Previous page: Pan-Seared Tuna with Ginger-Soy Vinaigrette

Palm Beach Citrus Halibut

D

SERVES: 4

𝒜 zesty light dish that is sure to delight. An easy family dinner that can be prepared with other mild white fish such as tilapia, sole, or snapper. Serve with Whipped Cauliflower Purée with Fresh Chives (see page 167).

Preheat oven to 375°F (190°C). Line a baking sheet with parchment paper.

Pat the fish dry with paper towels and set aside.

Finely crush the cereal and stir in the chopped parsley, orange zest, salt, tarragon and pepper. Transfer to a shallow dish.

Place the melted butter or oil in a shallow dish. Dip the fillets in the butter or oil, then coat with the cereal mixture. Place in a single layer on the prepared baking pan.

Bake uncovered without turning for 20 minutes or until the fish flakes easily with a fork. Garnish with orange slices.

Variation: Cornflakes or unseasoned bread crumbs can be substituted for Special K.

Chef's tip | WHEN HANDLING RAW FISH, IT IS BEST TO RESERVE A SEPARATE CUTTING BOARD FOR PREPARATION TO AVOID CROSS-CONTAMINATION.

1 pound (500 g) halibut fillets, fresh or frozen and thawed

2 cups (500 mL) Special K cereal

¼ cup (60 mL) finely chopped fresh flat-leaf parsley

½ teaspoon (2 mL) freshly grated orange zest

¼ teaspoon (1 mL) kosher salt

¼ teaspoon (1 mL) dry tarragon leaves, crushed

⅛ teaspoon (0.5 mL) freshly ground pepper

2 tablespoons (30 mL) melted unsalted butter or olive oil

1 orange, thinly sliced, for garnish

Pan-Seared Tuna
with Ginger-Soy Vinaigrette

SERVES: 4

Your guests will love this elegant and impressive dish that can be completely prepared in advance.

MARINADE

½ cup (125 mL) rice vinegar

¼ cup (60 mL) soy sauce

dash freshly ground pepper

¼ cup (60 mL) grated onion

1 teaspoon (5 mL) oil

1 tablespoon (15 mL) minced fresh ginger

TUNA

4 6-ounce (175-g) tuna steaks

1 tablespoon (15 mL) oil

VEGETABLES

⅔ cup (150 mL) julienned carrots

⅔ cup (150 mL) julienned celery

⅔ cup (150 mL) julienned cucumber

1 teaspoon (5 mL) oil

¼ teaspoon (1 mL) kosher salt

1 teaspoon (5 mL) freshly ground pepper

GARNISH

red onion slices

celery leaves

lemon slices

For the marinade, combine the rice vinegar, soy sauce, pepper, onion, oil and ginger in a small bowl.

Add the tuna and marinate for 20 minutes in the refrigerator.

Heat the tablespoon (15 mL) of oil in a large skillet. Sear the tuna for 3 minutes on each side or to the desired degree of doneness. Cut the tuna diagonally across the grain into thin slices.

For the vegetables, toss together the carrots, celery and cucumber in a small bowl.

Arrange ½ cup (125 mL) of the vegetable mixture on each plate and top with tuna slices. Drizzle each serving lightly with the teaspoon (5 mL) of oil, and sprinkle with salt and pepper.

Garnish with onion slices, celery leaves and lemon slices (optional).

Chef's tip | THE TERM "JULIENNE" MEANS TO CUT INTO LONG, THIN STRIPS OF EVEN WIDTH AND LENGTH.

Grilled Cedar-Planked Salmon

(P)

SERVES: 4

The cedar plank imparts a smoked flavour to your fish and the rustic aromas will transport your guests back to the woods. Cedar plank can be purchased at your local lumber store or kitchen store. Keep a spray water bottle close to your grill in case of emergencies.

Preheat grill until very hot and place the soaked plank on it. Close the lid and heat for 3–5 minutes, until the plank starts to crackle and smoke.

Meanwhile, pepper the fish and spread it with mustard, then sugar. Carefully lift the lid of the grill—it will be smoky. Salt the plank quickly and place the salmon on it. Close the lid and grill the salmon for 10–15 minutes. Check periodically to ensure the plank is not on fire; if it is, spray with a water bottle to extinguish flames.

Remove the plank with the salmon on top from the grill and allow it to cool for a few minutes on a nonflammable surface, like an old metal tray.

Serve the salmon directly from the plank or use a long flexible metal spatula to carefully transfer it to a serving platter.

Variation: You can marinate the fish beforehand with your favourite marinade.

1 untreated cedar plank*, soaked in water for 6 hours

freshly ground pepper

1 skinless Atlantic salmon fillet, about 1½ pounds (750 g)

¼ cup (60 mL) Dijon mustard

¼ cup (60 mL) packed brown sugar

1 tablespoon (15 mL) kosher salt

*About 1 inch (2.5 cm) thick, 12 inches (30 cm) long and 8 inches (20 cm) wide

Pepper-Crusted
Maple-Glazed Salmon

SERVES: 4

An elegant no-fuss classic. This can also be prepared with chicken or very firm tofu. In the summertime, grill the marinated fish directly over hot coals for about 3 minutes per side.

¾ cup (185 mL) pure maple syrup

¼ cup (60 mL) soy sauce

4 6-ounce (175-g) salmon fillets, skin removed

¼ cup (60 mL) coarsely ground pepper

½ teaspoon (2 mL) peanut or other vegetable oil, or a fine mist of oil spray

In a small deep bowl, or resealable plastic bag, mix together the maple syrup and soy sauce. Arrange the fillets so that the marinade completely covers the fish. Marinate in the refrigerator for 30–60 minutes.

Preheat oven to 400°F (200°C).

Line a baking sheet with aluminum foil. Rub oil over the foil.

Place the pepper on a small plate. Remove the salmon from the marinade and pat the top side only into the pepper to coat. Place the fillets, pepper side up, on the prepared baking sheet.

Bake on the top rack of the oven for 7 minutes. The syrup may cause the fish to smoke when cooking so don't be alarmed. If it starts to burn, loosely cover with foil.

Serve with Risotto Milanese (see page 154) and Oven-Roasted Asparagus (see page 168).

Broiled Indonesian Red Snapper

(D)

SERVES: 4

A soft-fleshed fish with bite! To increase or decrease the heat of the spice but maintain the flavour, add or reduce the amount of crushed red pepper.

Preheat broiler and position the rack 6 inches (15 cm) from the broiler.

In a small bowl, mash the garlic with the salt and pepper until a paste forms. Rub the snapper fillets with the paste.

In a saucepan, combine the soy sauce, lemon juice, brown sugar and crushed red pepper. Bring to a boil over high heat, stirring until the sugar dissolves.

Line a large rimmed baking sheet with foil. Brush with oil. Arrange the fillets on the baking sheet and pour half of the sauce over them. Broil for 8 minutes, or until the fillets are firm to the touch and opaque.

Transfer the fish to a platter or plates. Drizzle with the remaining sauce and the melted butter.

1 tablespoon (15 mL) minced garlic

½ teaspoon (2 mL) kosher salt

1 teaspoon (5 mL) freshly ground pepper

4 6– 8-ounce (175– 250-g) red snapper fillets, skinned

¼ cup (60 mL) soy sauce

3 tablespoons (45 mL) fresh lemon juice

2 tablespoons (30 mL) packed brown sugar

½ teaspoon (2 mL) crushed red pepper

vegetable oil, for brushing

2 tablespoons (30 mL) unsalted butter, melted

Tilapia with Basil Pesto
and Sun-Dried Tomatoes

Serves: 6

A mild sweet fish with tender flakes, tilapia (otherwise known as St. Peter's fish) can be raised to great culinary heights. You can prepare the sauce up to two days in advance. Spread it over the fish and broil immediately before serving.

Sauce

½ cup (125 mL) cream cheese

¼ cup (60 mL) mayonnaise

¼ cup (60 mL) oil-packed sun-dried tomatoes

¼ cup (60 mL) basil pesto (see page 141)

¼ cup (60 mL) finely chopped red onion

Fish

6 6–8-ounce (175–250-g) tilapia fillets

kosher salt

freshly ground pepper

Preheat broiler. Arrange the rack 6 inches (15 cm) from the top of the oven.

Process the cream cheese, mayonnaise, sun-dried tomatoes, pesto and onion in a food processor until smooth.

Spread some sauce on the bottom of an ovenproof baking dish. Place the fish in a single layer over the sauce. Season the fillets with salt and pepper on both sides. Spread the remaining sauce evenly over the fish.

Broil the fish for 8–12 minutes, or longer depending on the thickness of the fillets. The fish is cooked when the flesh is opaque.

Chef's tip | IF THE FILLETS ARE THINNER ON ONE END, SIMPLY CURL THE FISH UNDER ITSELF TO CREATE AN EVEN THICKNESS AND ENSURE EVEN COOKING

Basil Pesto

F D

MAKES: ABOUT 1 CUP (250 ML)

A classic Italian staple that is packed with flavour. Freeze leftover pesto in ice cube trays.

Purée the ingredients in a food processor until smooth. Store in a plastic container in the refrigerator for up to 1 week or in the freezer for up to 6 months.

Variations: Basil can be replaced with flat-leaf parsley or arugula and the pine nuts can be replaced with walnuts and pecans.

5 cloves garlic

2 cups (500 mL) fresh basil leaves

½ cup (125 mL) olive oil

¼ cup (60 mL) pine nuts, toasted, optional

¼ cup (60 mL) grated Parmesan cheese, optional

Sea Bass en Papillote

SERVES: 4

Very French, elegant and delicate in taste. The steam captured in the packet steams the fish while infusing it with the perfume of the herbs. Great for entertaining. The packets can be prepared and sealed in advance and kept in the refrigerator.

1 tablespoon (15 mL) olive oil

1 small onion, finely sliced

2 cups (500 mL) thinly sliced assorted mushrooms (white, cremini, portobello, shiitake, oyster, porcini)

kosher salt

freshly ground pepper

4 teaspoons (20 mL) unsalted butter

4 6-ounce (175-g) sea bass fillets

¼ cup (60 mL) white wine

4 sprigs fresh thyme

4 bay leaves, optional

Preheat oven to 450°F (230°C).

In a large skillet, heat the oil on medium heat. Sauté the onion for 1 minute, add the mushrooms and sauté for 2 minutes more. Season with salt and pepper and continue to cook until most of the liquid has evaporated. Set aside to cool.

Cut 2 16 x 12-inch (40 x 30-cm) pieces of aluminum foil. Fold in half to make 2 8 x 12-inch (20 x 30-cm) rectangles.

For each fillet, butter half a square of foil, then place a fillet on the buttered side and season with salt and pepper. Top each fillet with some mushrooms and onions, 1 tablespoon (15 mL) wine, a sprig of thyme and a bay leaf, if using.

Fold each fillet into a tightly sealed packet. Place the 4 packages on a baking sheet. Bake until the fish is opaque inside, about 12–15 minutes.

Set each package on a plate and open the packages carefully at the table for maximum effect, but be careful of the steam.

Variations: Trout, flounder or virtually any white firm-fleshed fish tastes especially delicious when cooked *en papillote.* ♦ Instead of mushrooms, use a combination of sun-dried tomatoes, spinach, carrots and zucchini along with fresh herbs and lemon to help flavour the fish.

Chef's tip | ALWAYS HAVE FISH PIECES OF EQUAL THICKNESS TO ENSURE EVEN COOKING. THE AVERAGE IS 1½ INCHES (7.5 CM) THICK DEPENDING ON THE SPECIES. CALCULATE ABOUT 10 MINUTES PER POUND FOR COOKING.

Snapper Puttanesca

SERVES: 2

A zesty and piquant low-calorie fish that is ready in minutes. Customarily this sauce is cooked but here it is simply assembled for faster results. This recipe can be easily doubled.

In a medium-sized bowl, combine the tomatoes, olives, capers, basil and pepper and let stand 15 minutes.

Preheat broiler with the rack 6 inches (15 cm) beneath the heat source.

Grease an 8-inch (2-L) square baking pan.

Place the fish fillets skin side down in the pan. Top with the puttanesca mixture, dividing equally over each fillet. Broil for about 5 minutes until the fish turns from translucent to opaque throughout.

Variations: Tilapia, flounder, sole, or any other white fish may also be used.

1 8-ounce (213-mL) can stewed tomatoes, coarsely chopped

2 tablespoons (30 mL) chopped, pitted kalamata olives

1 tablespoon (15 mL) drained capers

½ teaspoon (2 mL) dry basil

⅛ teaspoon (0.5 mL) freshly ground pepper

2 skinned red snapper fillets (about 6 ounces / 175 g each)

Ⓟ

Grilled Fish with
Peach Cilantro Salsa

Serves: 4

Gᴵ bold twist to enhance a fresh summer's catch! Jamaican jerk seasoning or Cajun seasoning can easily be found in the spice aisle of most grocery stores.

FISH

4 6-ounce (175-g) halibut, salmon, Chilean sea bass, or grouper fillets (each about 1 inch / 2.5 cm thick)

1 tablespoon (15 mL) olive oil

one of:

3 tablespoons (45 mL) Jamaican jerk seasoning

3 tablespoons (45 mL) Cajun seasoning

kosher salt and freshly ground pepper to taste

PEACH CILANTRO SALSA
MAKES: ABOUT 3½ CUPS (875 mL)

1½ cups (375 mL) finely diced peach

¾ cup (185 mL) finely diced red bell pepper

½ cup (125 mL) finely diced green bell pepper

½ cup (125 mL) finely diced onions

¼ cup (60 mL) chopped fresh cilantro

2 tablespoons (30 mL) fresh lemon juice

2 teaspoons (10 mL) olive oil

1 teaspoon (5 mL) minced garlic

kosher salt

freshly ground pepper

Oil grill rack and heat barbecue to medium-high heat.

Brush the fish with the oil. Spread the seasoning in a dish large enough to hold the fish. Dredge the fish in the seasoning, turning to coat. If using salt and pepper, simply sprinkle all over the fish.

Grill until the fish is opaque in the centre, about 4 minutes per side, turning once.

For the salsa, combine the peach, peppers, onions, cilantro, lemon juice, oil, garlic, salt and pepper in a large bowl and stir to blend. Prepare up to 1 day in advance to allow flavours to meld. Cover and refrigerate but bring to room temperature before serving with the fish.

Variations: Try using mangos or plums in place of the peaches. ♦ For a milder flavour, season the fish with kosher salt and freshly ground pepper.

Miso-Glazed Chilean Sea Bass

Ⓟ

Serves: 4

Miso is a naturally fermented soybean and grain purée that is aged up to 3 years. It comes in light and dark varieties and can be found in most Asian food stores. This recipe also works well with cod or salmon. Mirin is a sweet Japanese cooking wine.

In a saucepan, bring the sake or sherry and mirin to a boil. Boil for 20 seconds to evaporate the alcohol. Lower the heat, add the miso paste and stir with a wooden spoon to blend. When the miso has dissolved, raise the heat and add the sugar, stirring constantly. Remove from the heat once the sugar has completely dissolved.

Cool to room temperature.

Pat the fish fillets dry and place in a glass dish. Spread the marinade generously over the fish and cover with plastic wrap. Refrigerate for 1 hour.

Preheat oven to 400°F (200°C).

In an ovenproof skillet, heat the oil. Pan sear the fish on each side for 2 minutes until crispy, then finish in the oven for another 10–15 minutes. To test for doneness, pierce the fish with the top of a paring knife. The flesh should be opaque and flaky.

6 tablespoons (90 mL) sake or dry sherry
⅔ cup (150 mL) mirin (sweet Japanese cooking wine)
1 package (1 pound / 450 g) white miso paste
¾ cup (185 mL) sugar
4 6-ounce (175-g) sea bass fillets
2 teaspoons (10 mL) oil

Chef's tip | To ensure success, always look for the freshest fish available that day. Most white fish fillets are interchangeable.

Whole Fish Roasted in a Crust of Sea Salt

SERVES: 4

Easy preparation . . . dramatic presentation. Crack the hardened salt shell and behold the succulent red skinned snapper. The salt has a high water content. As the fish bakes, the salt becomes firmer and gradually encases the fish in a clay-like hermetic package.

FISH

1 3-pound (1.5-kg) whole sea bass or snapper, gutted but not scaled, head left on, tail and fins trimmed but not removed

4 pounds (2 kg) coarse sea salt or kosher salt

several sprigs fresh thyme

GARNISH

lemon wedges

extra-virgin olive oil

chopped fresh thyme

Preheat oven to 450°F (230°C).

Rinse the fish thoroughly inside and out and pat dry. Season the cavity with a little salt and tuck in a few sprigs of fresh thyme.

Evenly spread 1 pound (500 g) of the salt over the bottom of an ovenproof baking dish big enough to hold the fish without crowding it. Place the fish on top of the salt, and pour the remaining salt over the fish to cover it completely from head to tail. (If the fish is large, the tail may extend outside the baking dish.)

Place the fish in the centre of the oven and bake for 10 minutes per pound (500 g). Once cooked, remove the fish from the oven and allow it to sit for 3 minutes to firm up the flesh and make it easier to fillet. Brush away as much salt as possible so it will not fall into the flesh when you remove the skin. Using a sharp knife, gently scrape away and discard the skin from the top fillet of the fish. Remove and discard the thyme sprigs from the fish cavity.

Divide the top fillet along the centre bone into 2 pieces, removing any fat, extraneous flesh and skin. Using 2 large spoons, gently remove half of the fillet in neat pieces and then the other half. Still using the spoons, carefully remove and discard the centre bone. Divide the bottom fillet in 2 and remove the halves of the fillet in pieces.

Serve immediately, accompanied by lemon wedges and extra-virgin olive oil with chopped fresh thyme.

Baked Gefilte Fish Loaf

(P)

SERVES: 12–16

Similar to a meatloaf, this traditional favourite does not leave a fish odour as it bakes. This dish can be prepared up to three days in advance. Store in the refrigerator until needed.

Preheat oven to 325°F (165°C).

Grease a 9 x 5-inch (2-L) loaf pan or Bundt pan. Cut a piece of parchment or wax paper to fit the bottom of the pan and grease the paper.

In a skillet, heat the oil and sauté the onions on low heat until soft. Do not brown them—you want the fish mixture to remain white. Set aside.

In a large bowl, combine the sautéed onions with the minced fish. Divide the fish mixture evenly between 2 bowls. To each bowl add 1 egg and half of the ice water, carrots, salt, sugar and white pepper.

Put the contents of each bowl separately into a stand mixer with the paddle attachment. Mix for 10 minutes. This helps aerate the loaf. Leave some texture! Transfer both batches to a large bowl and stir in the matzo meal, horseradish and dill. Combine the two batches in a bowl. Spoon the fish into the prepared pan, spreading the top evenly.

Set the loaf pan in a large baking pan filled with about 2 inches (5 cm) of boiling water, a *bain-marie*. Bake for 50–60 minutes, or until the centre feels firm to the touch. Remove from the oven and cool for 1 hour.

Run a sharp knife around the sides and reverse the pan onto a platter. Remove the pan and paper. Refrigerate until needed.

To serve, slice and serve cold on a bed of romaine lettuce with cherry tomatoes and sliced cucumbers and, of course, horseradish *(chrain)*.

Chef's tip | ALWAYS STORE YOUR FISH IN THE BACK OF YOUR REFRIGERATOR WHERE IT IS COOLEST.

1 tablespoon (15 mL) vegetable oil

2 medium onions, coarsely chopped

3 pounds (1.5 kg) mixed minced fish, (whitefish, pickerel, doré)

2 large eggs

⅓ cup (75 mL) ice water

3 carrots, peeled and grated

1 tablespoon (15 mL) kosher salt

1 teaspoon (5 mL) sugar

½ teaspoon (2 mL) white pepper

2 tablespoons (30 mL) matzo meal

1 tablespoon (15 mL) prepared white horseradish

2–3 tablespoons (30–45 mL) chopped fresh dill

vegetarian

Previous page: Roasted Plum Tomato Sauce

Moussaka

D

SERVES: 6–8

An impressive soufflé-like dish that is layered with eggplant and Greek tradition. The eggplant is baked in a classic starch-based sauce called béchamel or white sauce.

Dust a 9 x 13-inch (3.5-L) casserole dish with the bread crumbs.

For the filling, season the potatoes with salt and pepper.

In a skillet, heat the oil on medium heat and sauté the onion until golden. Add the tomato sauce, veggie chuck and parsley and simmer for 10 minutes. Season with salt and pepper.

Layer the potatoes, eggplant and veggie ground round mixture in the casserole dish and repeat until it is filled to within ½ inch (1 cm) of the top. Let rest while preparing the béchamel sauce.

Preheat oven to 350°F (180°C).

For the béchamel sauce, melt butter or heat the olive oil in a medium saucepan. Add the flour and cook over low heat, stirring constantly. Do not let it brown. It will be pasty. Add the milk gradually and cook until thick, stirring occasionally.

Beat the egg yolks. Temper the yolks with a little of the warm sauce to keep them from scrambling. Add them to the saucepan and stir until thick. Add cayenne, if using, and stir.

In a separate bowl, beat the egg whites until stiff and gently fold them into the sauce. Pour over the vegetables and bake for 45–50 minutes. Remove from oven and let sit for 10 minutes to firm before cutting.

Chef's tips | TEMPERING EGG YOLKS MEANS ADDING A LITTLE OF THE WARM SAUCE TO THE EGGS WHILE MIXING, BEFORE ADDING THE EGGS TO THE MAIN POT OF WARM SAUCE. THIS KEEPS THE SAUCE FROM CURDLING.

VEGGIE GROUND ROUND IS A SOY-BASED PRODUCT THAT SIMULATES GROUND MEAT. IT IS AVAILABLE IN THE REFRIGERATOR SECTION IN THE GROCERY STORE.

¼ cup (60 mL) unseasoned bread crumbs

FILLING
3 medium Yukon gold potatoes, peeled and sliced into ½-inch (1-cm) rounds

kosher salt

freshly ground pepper

1 tablespoon (15 mL) olive oil

1 large onion, cut into small dice

1½ cups (375 mL) tomato sauce

1 6-ounce (175-g) package veggie ground round, rinsed under cold water

¼ cup (60 mL) chopped fresh flat-leaf parsley

1 large eggplant, peeled into ½-inch (1-cm) rounds

BÉCHAMEL SAUCE
¼ cup (60 mL) unsalted butter or olive oil

⅓ cup (75 mL) all-purpose flour

2 cups (500 mL) milk or soymilk

2 large eggs, separated

pinch cayenne pepper, optional

ⓕ ⓟ

Moroccan Tagine with Chickpeas

SERVES: 6–8

Tagine is a flavourful stew that is customarily prepared with chicken and 7 types of vegetables. To make an impression, pack prepared couscous into a tube pan and invert onto a serving platter. Fill the centre with warm tagine and garnish. Can be served hot or at room temperature.

2 teaspoons (10 mL) olive oil

1 cup (250 mL) finely diced onion

4 cloves garlic, minced

1 tablespoon (15 mL) chopped fresh ginger

1 teaspoon (5 mL) cardamom

1 teaspoon (5 mL) turmeric

½ teaspoon (2 mL) cumin

2 cups (500 mL) vegetable stock

2 cups (500 mL) peeled and diced parnsips

2 cups (500 mL) sweet potatoes, peeled and cut into chunks

2 carrots, peeled and cut into chunks

1 zucchini, cut into ½-inch (1-cm) half rounds

1 cinnamon stick

1 bay leaf

1 cup (250 mL) dates, pitted and sliced

1 19-ounce (540 mL) can chickpeas, drained and rinsed

6 plum (Roma) tomatoes, seeded and chopped

kosher salt and freshly ground pepper

2 tablespoons (30 mL) chopped fresh mint

2 tablespoons (30 mL) chopped fresh cilantro or flat-leaf parsley

½ cup (125 mL) slivered almonds, toasted

In a large skillet, heat the oil. Once hot, add the onion and sauté on medium-high heat for about 5 minutes or until translucent. Add the garlic and ginger and continue to sauté for 1 minute. Add the cardamom, turmeric and cumin and cook for 1 minute to bring out their flavours.

Add the stock with the parsnips, sweet potatoes, carrots, zucchini, cinnamon stick, bay leaf and dates and simmer, covered, for about 20 minutes. Stir in the chickpeas and tomatoes. Continue cooking, covered, for a further 10 minutes. Add more stock or water if the stew seems too dry.

Season with salt and pepper. Garnish with the chopped fresh mint, cilantro and toasted almonds right before serving.

Variations: Instead of dates, use currants, prunes, dried apricots or dried cranberries. ♦ Leftover stew can be puréed in the blender for a flavourful soup. Dilute with stock and garnish with some couscous and fresh herbs.

Penne with Sun-Dried Tomato Pesto

ⒻⒹ

SERVES: 4–6

Pesto is derived from the Italian word pestare, *which means to pound or to crush. It is a wonderful addition to have on hand to dress up pizzas, sauces and pasta (great as a ravioli filling!). Try spreading it over fish before grilling, or mix with mayonnaise for an interesting sandwich spread.*

For the pesto, soak the tomatoes in ¾ cup (185 mL) boiling water. Let stand for 10 minutes. Drain but reserve the soaking liquid.

Place the garlic in the food processor and mince. Scrape down bowl. Add the drained tomatoes, basil or parsley, 1 cup (250 mL) cheese and nuts. Purée until smooth. With the processor running, add the oil in a slow stream through the feed tube until the mixture becomes moist. If you find it too dry and you want to lower the fat content, add some of the reserved tomato soaking liquid. Season with salt and pepper.

The pesto keeps refrigerated for 1 week.

For the pasta, bring 12 cups (3 L) of water and the salt to a boil in a large pasta pot. Add the penne and cook until al dente, about 11 minutes. Drain but set aside 1–2 tablespoons (15–30 mL) of cooking liquid. While the penne is still warm, toss with about ½ cup (125 mL) of pesto to taste, and 1 tablespoon (15 mL) of the cooking liquid and mix until the noodles are evenly seasoned.

Garnish with chopped basil and grated Parmesan.

Freezing: This pesto can be frozen for up to 3 months in ice cube trays for individual portions.

Chef's tip | TOASTING NUTS BRINGS OUT THEIR FLAVOURS AND INCREASES SHELF LIFE. SIMPLY SPREAD THE NUTS OUT ON A BAKING SHEET AND TOAST THEM IN THE OVEN AT 350°F (180°C) FOR 5–7 MINUTES. WATCH THEM CAREFULLY BECAUSE THEY BURN EASILY. YOU CAN ALSO DO THIS IN YOUR TOASTER OVEN (MAKE SURE THE TOAST BUTTON IS SET TO LIGHT!).

SUN-DRIED TOMATO PESTO
MAKES: ABOUT 1 CUP (250 ML)

1 cup (250 mL) dry sun-dried tomatoes

2 cloves garlic

1 cup (250 mL) plus 2 tablespoons (15 mL) fresh basil leaves or flat-leaf parsley

1 cup (250 mL) plus ¼ cup (60 mL) freshly grated Parmesan cheese

½ cup (125 mL) pine nuts, walnuts or pecans, toasted

½–1 cup (125–250 mL) olive oil

kosher salt

freshly ground pepper

PASTA
1 teaspoon (5 mL) kosher salt

1 pound (500 g) penne pasta

GARNISH
chopped fresh basil

¼ cup (60 mL) freshly grated Parmesan cheese

Risotto Milanese

SERVES: 4

Arborio rice is a short-grain rice with a high starch content that releases a natural creaminess. Feel free to add favourite ingredients like mushrooms, squash, asparagus and/or fish. It tastes best when served immediately. Additional stock can be added to rehydrate the risotto if it becomes too thick.

4 cups (1 L) good quality vegetable stock

2 tablespoons (30 mL) unsalted butter or olive oil

½ cup (125 mL) minced onion

1 cup (250 mL) arborio rice

½ cup (125 mL) white wine

½–1 cup (125–250 mL) freshly grated Parmesan cheese

3 tablespoons (45 mL) chopped fresh flat-leaf parsley

kosher salt

freshly ground pepper

Bring the stock to a simmer in a heavy saucepan on medium heat.

In a separate large heavy bottomed saucepan, heat the butter or oil on medium-high heat. Sauté the onion until soft and translucent, about 5 minutes. Add the rice and sauté for another 2 minutes. Add the wine and stir until it has been absorbed.

Add 1 cup (250 mL) of stock and stir until it has been absorbed. Continue to add 1 cup (250 mL) of stock each time the previous addition has been absorbed by the rice. Stir constantly to ensure that the bottom does not burn. The rice should cook for 35–45 minutes, or until the rice is al dente.

Add the Parmesan cheese and parsley, and season with salt and pepper.

Variation: **MAKE-AHEAD RISOTTO:** Cook the risotto up to the stage of using 2 cups (500 mL) of stock. Remove the rice from the pan and spread on a baking sheet to cool. Refrigerate uncovered until the rice is cold.

To finish cooking the risotto, bring 1½ cups (375 mL) of stock to a boil. Place the chilled risotto in a large saucepan and add 2 tablespoons (30 mL) of butter or oil. Add the boiling stock and stir until the risotto creams up. Add the Parmesan and parsley. If the rice is too thick, add more stock. Serve immediately.

PANACHE | 154

Fresh Corn Spoon Bread

Ⓓ

SERVES: 6–8

A great way to celebrate summer. Separating the eggs adds a fluffy soufflé texture to this comfort dish. Serve with salad greens with Poppy Seed Dressing (see page 80).

Preheat oven to 375°F (190°C).

Butter an 8 x 8-inch (2-L) baking dish.

In a large heavy pot, mix together the milk, salt and pepper. Bring to a simmer and add the cornmeal gradually. Whisk continuously until the mixture comes to a boil. The mixture will thicken. Lower the temperature and continue to stir. It will be thick and bubbly. Keep stirring to prevent burning. Continue to stir for 15 minutes.

Transfer the mixture to a large mixing bowl and add the corn kernels, green onions and butter. Mix. Add the egg yolks, one at a time, and mix until blended.

In a separate bowl, beat the egg whites until firm. Gently fold the whites into the corn mixture. Spread the mixture evenly into the prepared pan and bake for 30 minutes until puffed and light golden brown. Serve immediately.

---

4 cups (1 L) milk

1½ teaspoons (7 mL) kosher salt

freshly ground pepper

1¼ cups (310 mL) coarse yellow cornmeal

1 cup (250 mL) corn kernels, fresh or frozen and thawed

6 green onions, both green and white parts, finely chopped

¼ cup (60 mL) unsalted butter, cut into pieces

3 large eggs, separated

Chef's tip | To REMOVE THE KERNELS FROM THE COB, STAND THE COBS UPRIGHT IN A SHALLOW BOWL WITH THE WIDER END DOWN. USING A SMALL KNIFE, SLICE DOWNWARD, TURNING THE COB AFTER EACH SLICE. THE KERNELS WILL FALL INTO THE BOWL ALONG WITH ANY SWEET JUICES FROM THE COB.

Polenta

The polenta can be made two days in advance wrapped in plastic and refrigerated. Once solidified and cooled, it can be cut into all sorts of shapes either with a knife or cookie cutters! Serve with Mushroom Ragout (see page 123) or warmed Eggplant Caponata (see page 28).

4 cups (1 L) water

2½ teaspoons (12 mL) kosher salt

1 cup (250 mL) coarse yellow cornmeal

Bring the water and salt to a boil in a heavy saucepan. Lower the heat so the water is just simmering. Gradually pour the cornmeal into the simmering water in a slow and steady stream. Stir almost continuously until all the cornmeal is absorbed. This takes about 2 minutes. The mixture will swell and become very thick.

Turn the heat to very low, then use a large wooden spoon to stir the cornmeal thoroughly in a figure 8 every 2–3 minutes. Be careful because it tends to pop back at you. The polenta is ready when it adheres to itself and pulls away from the sides of the pot, about 20–25 minutes.

Pour the polenta into a lightly greased 9 x13-inch (3.5-L) pan. (The polenta may be sticky so dip your spatula in water to reduce the stickiness!) Allow it to cool and solidify either at room temperature for 30 minutes, or in the refrigerator.

Variations: Experiment with different toppings. Try adding lots of interesting flavours to the polenta—goat cheese, herbs, roasted garlic and/ or sautéed shallots, for example. ♦ You can also grill the polenta. Simply cut the desired shape from the base. Brush both sides with olive oil. Grease the grill pan and heat to high. Place the polenta on the grill and cook for about 3 minutes each side.

Chef's tips | The secret to avoiding lumps in the polenta is to add the cornmeal gradually into the liquid.

Cornmeal is available in different grain sizes—use a coarse grain to provide texture for this dish.

Upscale Mac and Cheese

F D

SERVES: 6–8

Grown-up mac and cheese is fashionable in restaurants because it brings back memories of childhood comforts! Try preparing in individual ramekins to make guests feel more pampered. In addition, using blue cheese or goat cheese (chèvre) gives this dish real sophistication.

Butter a 3-quart (3-L) shallow baking dish.

For the topping, stir together the melted butter, bread crumbs and cheddar until well combined. This can be done 1 day ahead of time, covered and chilled.

Cook the macaroni in boiling water until al dente. Drain and rinse if preparing in advance.

Preheat oven to 400°F (200°C).

For the sauce, melt the butter over moderately low heat in a 5-quart (5-L) heavy saucepan and stir in the flour and red pepper flakes. Cook the roux, stirring, for 3 minutes. It will look pasty and dry. Slowly whisk in the milk and the cream.

Bring the sauce to a boil, whisking constantly, then lower to simmer and whisk occasionally, for 3 minutes. Stir in the cheese, mustard, salt and pepper. Remove the pan from heat. Add the macaroni and combine. Transfer to a baking dish.

Sprinkle the topping evenly over the macaroni and bake in the centre of the oven for 20–25 minutes, or until golden and bubbling.

Variation: Instead of one big baking dish, try using 6–8 individual ramekins (depending on their size) and adjust baking time.

Chef's tip | TO MAKE BREAD CRUMBS, PLACE TOAST OR DRIED-OUT BREAD IN A FOOD PROCESSOR AND PULSE A FEW TIMES. BREAD CRUMBS CAN BE KEPT FROZEN IN A RESEALABLE PLASTIC BAG.

TOPPING

2 tablespoons (30 mL) unsalted butter, melted

2 cups (500 mL) coarse dry unseasoned bread crumbs

1 cup (250 mL) coarsely grated extra-sharp cheddar cheese (about 4 ounces / 125 g)

PASTA

1 pound (500 g) elbow macaroni

CHEESE SAUCE

3 tablespoons (45 mL) unsalted butter

3 tablespoons (45 mL) all-purpose flour

½ teaspoon (2 mL) dry hot red pepper flakes

2¾ cups (685 mL) milk

¾ cup (185 mL) heavy cream (35%)

4 cups (1 L) coarsely grated extra-sharp cheddar (mix of orange and yellow, about 1 pound / 500 g)

2 teaspoons (10 mL) Dijon mustard

1½ teaspoons (7 mL) kosher salt

¼ teaspoon (1 mL) freshly ground pepper

Texan-Style Chili

SERVES: 8–10

Perfect for a comforting Sunday night dinner with close friends and family. Canned beans are a useful staple to keep in your pantry for quick nutritious meals.

2 tablespoons (30 mL) olive oil

1 large onion, cut into small dice

1 russet potato, peeled and cut into ½-inch (1-cm) cubes

3 cloves garlic, chopped

1½ 12-ounce (375- g) packages veggie ground round, rinsed and drained or ¾ pound (375 g) frozen firm tofu, drained and crumbled

2 tablespoons (30 mL) chili powder

½ teaspoon (2 mL) cumin

1 teaspoon (5 mL) cayenne powder

2 tablespoons (30 mL) tomato paste

2 28-ounce (796-mL) cans diced or whole tomatoes

1 19-ounce (540-mL) can lentils, rinsed and drained

1 14-ounce (398-mL) can white or black beans, rinsed and drained

1 cup (250 mL) fresh or frozen corn kernels

1 jalapeño pepper (pith removed), finely chopped

kosher salt

freshly ground pepper

chopped fresh cilantro

shredded Monterey Jack cheese

sour cream

In a large pan, heat the oil and sauté the onion and potato until golden, about 7 minutes. Add the garlic, the ground round or tofu and the spices and cook for 2–3 minutes. Add the tomato paste and tomatoes. Bring to a boil and add the lentils, beans, corn, and jalapeño. Season with salt and pepper.

Reduce heat and simmer, covered, for 10 minutes. Remove the lid and simmer for another 40 minutes to 1 hour. If the chili becomes too thick, add water.

Garnish with chopped cilantro, shredded cheese and sour cream.

Chef's tip | IF USING TOFU, FREEZE AND THAW. SQUEEZE OUT THE MOISTURE AND CRUMBLE INTO PIECES. USE AS DIRECTED IN THE RECIPE. THE TOFU WILL HAVE THE TEXTURE OF GROUND BEEF.

Sweet Potato Quesadillas

(D)

SERVES: 6

beautiful and nutritious adaptation of a Mexican favourite. The whipped sweet potato and Monterey Jack cheese is sandwiched between 2 tortillas that are toasted in the oven for a delightful light lunch or hors d'oeuvre.

Preheat oven to 400°F (200°C).

Line 2 baking sheets with parchment paper or lightly greased aluminum foil.

Heat the oil in a small skillet. Add the onions and sauté until translucent, about 5 minutes. Add the garlic and cook for 1 minute. Cool.

Scoop out the flesh from the sweet potato and put in the food processor. Add the sautéed onion and garlic and purée. Add the sour cream and mix. Season to taste with salt and pepper.

On the baking sheet, evenly spread 1 tortilla with ¼ cup (60 mL) of potato mixture. Sprinkle with cheese and cover with another tortilla. Repeat with the remaining tortillas. Bake in the oven for about 7–10 minutes, or until the cheese melts and the tortilla is crispy.

Cut into wedges and eat with sour cream and salsa.

Variation: Experiment with different fillings like grilled vegetables, hummus, a variety of cheeses or roasted garlic.

1 teaspoon (5 mL) olive oil

1 medium onion, cut into small dice

2 cloves garlic, minced

2 pounds (1 kg) sweet potatoes, baked whole

2 tablespoons (30 mL) sour cream

kosher salt

freshly ground pepper

12 10-inch (25-cm) whole wheat flour tortillas

1 cup (250 mL) grated Monterey Jack or mozzarella cheese

sour cream or pressed yogurt (see page 26)

salsa

Mushroom and Black Bean Burritos

Ⓓ

SERVES: 6

An easy-to-assemble Mexican favourite that is truly divine with fresh Guacamole (see page 27) and a margarita! Cremini mushrooms are also referred to as babybella mushrooms.

2 tablespoons (30 mL) olive oil

2 medium onions, finely sliced

2 red bell peppers, julienned

3 cloves garlic, crushed

20 ounces (650 g) cremini and button mushrooms, sliced

1 tablespoon (15 mL) chili powder

1 15-ounce (398-mL) can black beans, drained and rinsed

½ cup (125 mL) chopped fresh cilantro

¾ cup (175 mL) green or red salsa

kosher salt

freshly ground pepper

6 9- or 10-inch (23- or 25-cm) flour tortillas

6 tablespoons (90 mL) crumbled goat cheese

Preheat oven to 350°F (180°C).

In a large nonstick skillet, heat 1 tablespoon (15 mL) of the oil on medium heat, and sauté the onions, bell peppers and garlic until lightly brown, about 15 minutes.

Add the remaining oil, the mushrooms and chili powder, and cook until the juice from the mushrooms evaporates. Add the beans, cilantro and salsa, and cook for another 3 minutes. Season with salt and pepper.

Wrap the tortillas with aluminum foil and warm in the oven for 15 minutes. Divide the mushroom mixture equally among the 6 warm tortillas. Sprinkle with the goat cheese, fold in 2 sides of the tortillas, then roll up to enclose the filling. Serve immediately.

Chef's tip | CILANTRO, ALSO KNOWN AS CORIANDER (ESPECIALLY IN ITS DRY FORM), IS AN HERB THAT IS COMMON IN MEXICAN AND THAI CUISINE. OFTEN MISTAKEN FOR ITALIAN FLAT-LEAF PARSLEY, CILANTRO HAS A FRESH AND DISTINCTIVE FLAVOUR AND AROMA.

Fasoulia

SERVES: 8–10

A Greek specialty of giant lima beans (also known as butter beans) bathed in fresh tomatoes, parsley and garlic. It can be served hot or at room temperature and is a meal in itself when served with fluffy rice. Also good with grilled fish or as a buffet dish.

In a large bowl, soak the beans overnight in water.

Drain and rinse the beans. Place them in a large pot and cover with 16 cups (4 L) of water. Bring to a boil and cook for 25 minutes or until soft. Drain.

Preheat oven to 350°F (180°C).

In a 3-quart (3-L) baking dish, combine the tomatoes, tomato paste, parsley, garlic and onion. Add the olive oil, lima beans, water and salt and pepper. Stir together. Bake, covered, for 2 hours.

Chef's tips | IF YOU FORGOT TO SOAK YOUR BEANS OVERNIGHT, FILL A POT WITH LOTS OF WATER AND ADD THE BEANS. BRING TO A BOIL AND TURN OFF THE HEAT. LET SIT, COVERED, FOR 1 HOUR. RINSE THE BEANS AND COVER WITH 16 CUPS (4 L) OF FRESH WATER. COOK AS DIRECTED.

FREEZE LEFTOVER TOMATO PASTE EITHER IN A LOG IN PLASTIC WRAP OR FLASH FREEZE IN ICE CUBE TRAYS. KEEP IN RESEALABLE BAGS IN THE FREEZER.

1 pound (500 g) jumbo lima beans

6 large tomatoes, peeled and chopped or 1 28–ounce (796-mL) can diced tomatoes

2½ tablespoons (37 mL) tomato paste

1 bunch fresh flat-leaf parsley, chopped (1 cup / 250 mL)

1 clove garlic, minced

1 cup (250 mL) chopped onion

1 cup (250 mL) olive oil

1 cup (250 mL) water

3–4 teaspoons (15–20 mL) kosher salt

½ teaspoon (2 mL) freshly ground pepper

Roasted Plum Tomato Sauce

FP

Perfect for pizzas, pastas or as a stand-alone condiment, this quick and easy roasted sauce brings out the natural sweetness of the tomatoes. When fresh tomatoes are unavailable, you will have good results using canned tomatoes for consistently good flavour.

2 pounds (1 kg) plum (Roma) tomatoes, cored and quartered

1 large onion, cut into wedges

2 cloves garlic

1 tablespoon (15 mL) olive oil

1 tablespoon (15 mL) dry oregano

1 teaspoon (5 mL) kosher salt

½ teaspoon (2 mL) freshly ground pepper

1 tablespoon (15 mL) balsamic vinegar

1 tablespoon (15 mL) chopped fresh basil

In a medium bowl, toss together the tomatoes, onion, garlic, olive oil, oregano, salt and pepper. Marinate for at least 10 minutes or up to an hour to allow some of the juices to be drawn out of the tomatoes.

Preheat oven to 400°F (200°C).

Transfer the vegetables from the marinade into a 9 x 13-inch (3.5-L) baking dish and roast, uncovered, for 30 minutes. The tomato skins should loosen and begin to brown.

Transfer the mixture to a food processor and pulse until the mixture is coarsely chopped. Season with balsamic vinegar, chopped basil and more salt and pepper.

Serve immediately as a topping for Polenta (see page 156) or with a bowl of hot pasta.

on the side

Previous page: Oven-Roasted Beets with Crumbled Goat Cheese and Chives

Oven-Roasted Beets
with Crumbled Goat Cheese and Chives

Ⓓ

SERVES: 4

Cooking beets in the oven caramelizes their sugars without the mess of boiling. Reserve the leafy stems and blanch and sauté with fresh garlic for added nutrition! Omit the goat cheese for a pareve dish.

Preheat oven to 350°F (180°C).

Wash the beets and wrap them in aluminum foil. Bake for about 1½ hours or until tender. Cool in the aluminum foil.

Peel the beets when cool by just rubbing the skins off with your fingers. Cut beets into quarters. Gently toss with the lemon juice and olive oil. Season with salt and pepper.

Garnish with the chives and goat cheese

Variations: Look in the market for different varieties of beets to add an interesting colour dimension to your dish.

2 pounds (1 kg) beets (about 6), with 1 inch (2.5 cm) of stem

juice of 1 lemon

2 tablespoons (30 mL) extra-virgin olive oil

kosher salt

freshly ground pepper

1–2 tablespoons (15–30 mL) chopped fresh chives, for garnish

½ cup (125 mL) crumbled goat cheese, for garnish

Chef's tip | TO REMOVE BEET STAINS FROM HANDS AND CUTTING BOARDS, SPRINKLE THE STAINED AREA WITH SALT, RINSE, AND THEN SCRUB WITH SOAP. THE SALT CRYSTALS HELP DRAW THE BEET JUICES OUT.

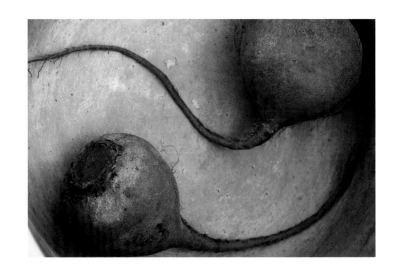

Oven-Fried Zucchini

SERVES: 6

The crispness of the batter complements the tender zucchini. They taste like a fritter but without the grease. Best right out of the oven, people will finish them as quickly as they are ready.

1 cup (250 mL) all-purpose flour

1 cup (250 mL) water

2 tablespoons (30 mL) olive oil

1 teaspoon (5 mL) kosher salt

freshly ground pepper

2 large egg whites

4 zucchini or yellow squash, washed and dried well and sliced on a diagonal into ⅛-inch (3-mm) slices

Preheat oven to 450°F (230°C).

Line a large baking sheet with parchment paper.

In a bowl, prepare the batter by mixing together the flour, water, oil, salt and pepper. Let stand for 20 minutes.

In the meantime, beat the egg whites until they form soft peaks. Fold them gently into the batter.

Dip the zucchini or squash into the batter to coat, or place the batter in a large resealable plastic bag, add the vegetables and toss to fully coat them. Place them on the prepared baking pan in a single layer to ensure crispness. Bake for about 12 minutes or until browned, then flip over and bake for another 2 minutes.

Variations: Eggplant, broccoli, cauliflower and mushrooms can all be used instead of the zucchini to create a medley. Simply adjust the cooking time accordingly.

Whipped Cauliflower Purée with Fresh Chives

SERVES: 4

For those on low-carb diets, this dish can replace mashed potatoes. Serve a mound on a plate topped with a piece of broiled fish. Can be prepared earlier in the day and reheated in the microwave or conventional oven.

In a large saucepan, combine the cauliflower, water and salt over high heat. Bring to a boil, then reduce the heat to medium and cook until the cauliflower is very soft, about 30 minutes.

Remove from the heat and drain. Put the cauliflower, olive oil, vegetable stock and cream or milk, if using, in a food processor and purée until smooth. Season with salt and white pepper.

Garnish with fresh chives.

½ pound (250 g) cauliflower florets, stems trimmed

3 cups (750 mL) water

kosher salt

1 tablespoon (15 mL) olive oil

⅓ cup (75 mL) vegetable stock

1–2 tablespoons (15–30 mL) heavy (35%) cream or milk, optional

white pepper

2 tablespoons (30 mL) chopped fresh chives

Oven-Roasted Asparagus

Serves: 4

Add to any antipasto platter, frittata or salad—these are so good there may be none left when it comes time to put them on the platter!

2 pounds (1 kg) asparagus, stems trimmed

2 tablespoons (30 mL) olive oil

kosher salt

freshly ground pepper

Preheat oven to 400°F (200°C).

Line a baking sheet with a silpat mat or parchment paper.

In a large bowl, toss the asparagus with the oil and add salt and pepper to taste. Spread the asparagus in a single layer on the baking sheet.

Place in the oven and roast until the asparagus is vibrant green, soft and starting to wrinkle, about 10 minutes, depending on thickness.

Serve warm or at room temperature.

Variation: Trimmed green beans, Brussels sprouts and broccoli can all take the place of the asparagus. Just remember that all the vegetables should be cut the same size to ensure even cooking. Reduce the cooking time for thinner vegetables such as green beans.

Chef's tip | To snap the tough ends off the asparagus, hold the spear about 1 inch (2 cm) up from the bottom. Bend the spear until it snaps.

Spinach Soufflé

M

SERVES: 6–8

Do not be intimidated by the thought of separating eggs. It is easiest to do when the eggs are cold. The spinach mixture can be prepared earlier in the day and kept in the refrigerator. Remember to serve soufflé straight from the oven.

Preheat oven to 325°F (160°C).

Grease an 8-cup (2-L) soufflé dish.

In a bowl, mix the egg yolks with the nutmeg and spinach.

In a large skillet, heat the oil on medium heat. Add the onion and sauté for 3 minutes. Stir in the flour and blend. Add the stock and stir to prepare the sauce.

When the sauce comes to a boil, add the spinach mixture. Reduce the heat immediately. Cook, stirring, for 1 minute to allow the eggs to thicken. Season with salt and pepper. Set aside and cool.

In a clean bowl, beat the egg whites until stiff. Fold the egg whites into the cooled spinach mixture. Mix gently until well incorporated. Transfer the mixture into the prepared soufflé dish and bake for 45 minutes or until firm. Serve immediately.

6 large eggs, separated
pinch freshly grated nutmeg
2 10-ounce (300-g) packages chopped frozen spinach, thawed and squeezed dry
6 tablespoons (90 mL) oil
1 small onion, cut into small dice
6 tablespoons (90 mL) all-purpose flour
2 cups (500 mL) chicken stock
½ teaspoon (2 mL) kosher salt
¼ teaspoon (1 mL) freshly ground pepper

Chef's tips | ALWAYS WHIP EGG WHITES WHEN THEY ARE AT ROOM TEMPERATURE FOR GREATEST VOLUME.

NUTMEG CAN BE BOUGHT AS A WHOLE NUT AND GRATED AS NEEDED FOR MAXIMUM FLAVOUR. A LITTLE GOES A LONG WAY.

Sautéed Broccoli Rabe

Ⓟ

SERVES: 4

A tangy Italian green also known as rapini. It is wonderful in pastas or on its own.

1½ pounds (750 g) broccoli rabe
1 tablespoon (15 mL) olive oil
1 clove garlic, minced
pinch red pepper flakes
kosher salt
freshly ground pepper

Trim the stalks of the broccoli rabe with a paring knife, keeping the leaves and florets attached.

In a large pot of boiling water, blanch the rabe for 60 seconds or until it is bright green. This helps remove some of the bitterness. Remove from the pot and run under cold water to stop the cooking. Drain.

In a large skillet, heat the oil on medium-high heat. Add the garlic and red pepper flakes and sauté for 1 minute to infuse. Add the drained rabe and toss with the flavoured oil. Season with salt and pepper.

Serve immediately.

Variation: Broccoli also works well in this recipe.

Sautéed Bok Choy
with Ginger and Enoki Mushrooms

Ⓟ

SERVES: 4

Ɛnoki mushrooms are delicate Japanese mushrooms that have tiny tips and skinny stems. Choose ones that are white and crisp and cut away the brown section at the base.

Heat the oil in a large sauté pan on high heat. Add the onion, garlic and ginger and sauté until the mixture begins to soften, about 3 minutes. Add the bok choy and the mushrooms and sauté until they are cooked through, about 5–8 minutes.

Season to taste with salt and pepper. Serve warm.

5 tablespoons (75 mL) olive or grapeseed oil

1 small red onion, chopped

2 cloves garlic, chopped

5 tablespoons (75 mL) grated fresh ginger

8 whole baby bok choy, roughly chopped

2 bunches enoki mushrooms, trimmed or 1 cup (250 mL) sliced shiitake mushrooms

kosher salt

freshly ground pepper

Brussels Sprouts with Pecans

SERVES: 8

Sliced Brussels sprouts sautéed into tender greens is a wonderful addition to any Thanksgiving table. This dish can be prepared in advance and reheated in the oven.

2 teaspoons (10 mL) olive oil

1 cup (250 mL) chopped onions

4 cloves garlic, thinly sliced

8 cups (2 L) Brussels sprouts, halved and thinly sliced, about 1½ pounds (750 g)

½ cup (125 mL) chicken stock

1½ teaspoons (7 mL) sugar

½ teaspoon (2 mL) kosher salt

2–3 tablespoons (30–45 mL) coarsely chopped pecans, toasted

Heat the oil in a large nonstick skillet over medium-high heat. Add the onions and garlic and sauté for 4 minutes or until lightly browned. Stir in the Brussels sprouts and sauté for 2 minutes.

Add the chicken stock and sugar and cook partially covered for 5 minutes or until the liquid evaporates, stirring frequently. Season with salt.

Sprinkle with pecans and serve.

Variation: To make this a dairy dish, use vegetable stock and, if desired, butter instead of oil.

Szechwan Green Beans

(P)

Grapeseed oil is a flavourless oil that has the benefit of having a high smoking point and being healthful. It pairs well with the toasted sesame oil, which burns easily but has intense flavour.

Place a wok or large heavy deep skillet over medium-high heat.

When hot, about 1 minute, add both oils and the red pepper flakes. Add the green beans immediately. (It is vital that the beans are completely dry when added to the oil to avoid flare-ups and burning!)

Turn the heat to high and stir-fry until the beans are seared, about 5 minutes. Add the garlic and salt. Stir-fry for 1 minute longer and remove from the heat.

Serve hot, warm or at room temperature.

2 tablespoons (30 mL) grapeseed oil

2 tablespoons (30 mL) toasted sesame oil

pinch of crushed red pepper flakes

2 pounds (1 kg) green beans, washed, trimmed and dried

8 cloves garlic, minced

½ teaspoon (2 mL) kosher salt

Sweet Potato Mash

SERVES: 4

southern take on mashed potatoes. The combination of sweet and white potatoes adds a lightness to the mash that is irresistible. It will keep for two to three days if refrigerated. Reheat in the microwave for five to six minutes, stirring halfway through the heating time.

2 large sweet potatoes

1 white Idaho potato (about the size of your fist)

2 tablespoons (30 mL) unsalted butter or margarine

1 teaspoon (5 mL) minced garlic

1½ tablespoons (22 mL) Jack Daniels or any preferred bourbon

kosher salt

freshly ground pepper

Peel all the potatoes and cut them into even pieces.

Place the potatoes in a pot of cold water and bring to a boil. Cook until tender.

Drain the potatoes and return them to the pot. Any remaining moisture on the potatoes will help keep the mash moist.

Add the butter or margarine, garlic and bourbon, then mash the potatoes until almost smooth. A few chunks will give the mash a pleasant texture.

Season with salt and pepper.

Roasted New Potatoes with Rosemary and Garlic

SERVES: 4–6

An easy favourite at any time of the year. For an interesting twist, add carrots, parsnips, red onions and sweet potatoes. They bring a natural sweetness to the dish!

Preheat oven to 425°F (220°C).

Line a baking sheet with aluminum foil.

Place the quartered potatoes in a medium-size bowl. Toss with the oil, paprika, salt and pepper. Spread on a baking sheet and place in the preheated oven. Do not overlap the potatoes or they will steam and not crisp.

After 25 minutes, shake the potatoes around and add the rosemary and chopped garlic. Bake for another 10–15 minutes. If you like your potatoes extra crispy, keep them in the oven longer, but watch them so they do not burn!

Garnish with chopped parsley.

Variations: Fingerlings, Yukon gold, Peruvian or new potatoes can also be used. ♦ Dress the potatoes up by tossing them with freshly grated Parmesan cheese just before serving.

6 large red potatoes, washed and quartered but unpeeled

1 tablespoon (15 mL) olive oil

2 teaspoons (10 mL) paprika

1 teaspoon (5 mL) kosher salt

pinch freshly ground pepper

1 tablespoon (15 mL) fresh rosemary or 1 teaspoon (5 mL) dry rosemary

2–3 cloves garlic, minced

2–3 tablespoons (30–45 mL) chopped fresh flat-leaf parsley, for garnish

Mashed Potatoes
with Green Onion Pesto

SERVES: 6

Pesto can be made with just about any herb and provides deep flavour. Remember that a scallion is the same thing as a green onion and should not be mistaken for a dry shallot. The mashed potatoes may be prepared earlier in the day. Reheat in the microwave and then fold in the pesto.

POTATOES

2 pounds (1 kg) potatoes, preferably Yukon gold, peeled and sliced into large pieces

¼ cup (60 mL) milk or soy milk

1 teaspoon (5 mL) kosher salt

GREEN ONION PESTO
MAKES: ABOUT ⅔ CUP (150 mL)

⅓ cup (75 mL) sliced green onions, both green and white parts

2 teaspoons (10 mL) grated fresh ginger

¼ teaspoon (1 mL) kosher salt

⅓ cup (75 mL) canola oil or grapeseed oil

Boil the potatoes in lightly salted water until tender. Remove potatoes from water, saving ½ cup (125 mL) of potato water for possible use later on (see Variation below).

Mash potatoes until smooth with either a ricer or a potato masher. Never mash potatoes in the food processor—they will become rubbery.

Heat the milk and salt in the microwave on high power for 1 minute or heat on the stovetop, stirring to dissolve the salt. Combine with the potatoes.

For the pesto, combine the green onion, ginger, salt and oil in a food processor until smooth (may be prepared 1 day ahead).

Fold ¼ cup (60 mL) of the pesto into the mashed potatoes and serve hot.

Freeze remaining pesto in an ice cube tray.

Variation: Substitute ½ cup (125 mL) of potato water for the milk for a pareve version.

Chef's tip | A RICER IS A KITCHEN TOOL THAT MAKES SMOOTH MASHED POTATOES.

Lacy Potato Latkes

ⓕ ⓟ

SERVES: 6

𝒜 Hanukkah specialty that can be enjoyed all year round. Try adding some grated sweet potato to the potatoes to give colour and added nutrition to these festive pancakes. Delicious served with Chunky Homemade Applesauce (see page 206).

Peel the potatoes and grate them coarsely by hand or in the food processor. Put them in a bowl of water as you work to prevent blackening. Drain and squeeze all the liquid from the potatoes.

Transfer the grated potatoes and onion to a bowl and add the eggs, flour, salt and pepper. Mix well.

To a large skillet, add oil to a depth of ¼ inch (6 mm). Heat oil on medium-high heat. When the oil is hot, add the batter by heaping tablespoonfuls, or even more depending on how big you like your pancakes. Cook until golden, about 3–5 minutes per side depending on the thickness. Flip and cook for another 3–5 minutes. Repeat with remaing batter, adding more oil as needed.

Remove latkes to a plate lined with paper towels to absorb excess oil. Repeat with remaining batter.

Keep warm in a low temperature (300°F / 150°C) preheated oven, or, if made in advance, reheat in one layer at 400°F (200°C).

Variation: Make smaller latkes for a tasty hors d'oeuvre served with Crème Fraîche (see page 53) and smoked salmon.

2 pounds (1 kg) Yukon gold, Idaho or russet potatoes
1 medium onion, grated
2 large eggs, beaten
3 tablespoons (45 mL) all-purpose flour
½ tablespoon (7 mL) kosher salt
¼ teaspoon (1 mL) freshly ground pepper
oil for sautéing

Scalloped Potatoes
with Caramelized Onions

SERVES: 4–6

A light version of scalloped potatoes without the cream. Easily prepared in advance and reheated. Be patient when caramelizing onions—allow time for the natural sugars to release from the onion to enrich the flavour.

1 tablespoon (15 mL) unsalted butter

2 large onions, thinly sliced (4 cups / 1 L)

6 Yukon gold potatoes, peeled and thinly sliced (5–6 cups / 1.25–1.5 L)

kosher salt

freshly ground pepper

½ cup (125 mL) grated Gruyère cheese

Preheat oven to 375°F (190°C). Lightly grease a 9 x 13-inch (3.5-L) baking dish.

In a large skillet, melt the butter. Add the sliced onions and cook on medium heat for about 30 minutes until caramelized, stirring occasionally. Set aside.

Spread 1 layer of potatoes in the baking dish and sprinkle with some salt and pepper. Add a layer of onions and then some cheese. Repeat, ending with the cheese on top.

Bake for about 1 hour or until browned on top.

Chef's tips | ALWAYS STORE POTATOES IN A DARK COOL PLACE LIKE A DRAWER OR INSIDE A PAPER (NOT PLASTIC) BAG.

USING A MANDOLIN PRODUCES EVEN, THIN SLICES, WHICH REDUCES COOKING TIME AND IMPROVES THE FINAL LOOK OF THE DISH.

Mushroom Barley Pilaf

Ⓓ

SERVES: 6

A risotto method of cooking using an ancient grain. To make this dish pareve, replace the butter with margarine and omit the Parmesan.

Heat the oil in a large skillet on medium-high heat. Add the barley and stir until it is lightly toasted. Add the garlic, green onions, rosemary and mushrooms and sauté for 3 minutes. Add ½ cup (125 mL) of the stock or water and cook for 1 minute. Let the barley absorb the liquid.

Add ½ cup (125 mL) of stock every 5 minutes or until absorbed, and cook until the barley is tender. Keep stirring.

Add the Parmesan cheese, butter, salt and pepper. Garnish with chives and serve immediately.

Variation: If in a rush, you can substitute Israeli couscous for the barley. It takes less time to cook and you may not need all the stock.

1 tablespoon (15 mL) olive oil

1 cup (250 mL) pearl barley

2 cloves garlic, chopped

2 green onions, both white and green parts, sliced

1 teaspoon (5 mL) dry rosemary

2½ cups (625 mL) mushroom, sliced

3 cups (750 mL) vegetable stock or water

2 teaspoons (10 mL) grated Parmesan cheese

2 teaspoons (10 mL) unsalted butter

kosher salt

freshly ground pepper

1 tablespoon (15 mL) chopped fresh chives, for garnish

Rice with Vermicelli, Green Onions and Garlic

SERVES: 4

A tasty way to make a simple rice dish with very few ingredients. Always wash long-grain rice to remove additional starch. The rice is cleaned when the water is no longer cloudy.

2 tablespoons (30 mL) olive oil

2 ounces (60 g), about 10 threads, angel hair pasta, broken into 2-inch (5-cm) pieces

1 cup (250 mL) long-grain white rice

¼ cup (60 mL) sliced green onion, white part only

2 cloves garlic, minced

2 cups (500 mL) vegetable stock or water

1 teaspoon (5 mL) kosher salt

Heat the oil in a 2–3 quart (2–3 L) heavy saucepan over moderately high heat until hot but not smoking. Sauté the pasta pieces, stirring constantly, until browned. The pasta will have a nutty smell.

Add the rice and sauté, stirring, until coated with oil, about 2 minutes. Stir in the green onions and garlic and sauté until golden, about 1 minute. Add the stock or water and salt and bring to a boil. Reduce the heat to low and cook, covered, until the liquid is absorbed, about 15 minutes.

Remove the rice from the heat and fluff with a fork, then let stand, covered, for 5 minutes.

Variation: If using brown rice, adjust the liquid and cooking time according to the package directions.

Basmati Rice with Saffron and Golden Raisins

SERVES: 4

Saffron comes from the dried stigmas of the crocus plant and remains the world's most expensive spice. Crumble the threads of saffron to release the flavours and aroma. When steeped in liquid, the crushed threads release a golden hue.

Heat the oil in a medium-size pot. Add the onion and sauté until soft. Add the rice and sauté for 1 minute.

Add the water, cardamom pods, saffron, raisins, salt and sugar. Bring to a boil, cover and reduce heat to a simmer. Do not stir. Cook for about 15 minutes. Turn off the heat and let the rice rest, covered, for 10 minutes to steam.

Fluff with a fork, mix in the pine nuts and serve.

Chef's tip | CARDAMOM PODS, NATIVE TO INDIA AND AVAILABLE AT ASIAN MARKETS, ARE AROMATIC GREEN PODS WITH A SWEET AND SPICY FLAVOUR.

1 teaspoon (5 mL) olive oil

½ cup (125 mL) diced red onion

1 cup (250 mL) white basmati rice, rinsed

2 cups (500 mL) water

3 cardamom pods

¼ teaspoon (1 mL) saffron threads, crushed

2 tablespoons (30 mL) golden raisins

¾ teaspoon (4 mL) kosher salt

1 teaspoon (5 mL) sugar

¼ cup (60 mL) toasted pine nuts

desserts

Previous page: Rustic Plum Galette

Lemon Soufflé

Ⓓ

Serves: 6–8

A nice light and refreshing dessert! Use freshly squeezed lemon juice to maximize the flavour. Serve with Raspberry Coulis (see page 208) for a beautiful effect.

Preheat oven to 375°F (190°C).

Butter an 8-cup (2-L) soufflé dish and sprinkle with sugar.

In a pot, melt the butter with the lemon juice and 1 cup (250 mL) of the sugar. Remove from heat. Pour the egg yolks into the hot butter and lemon mixture and stir with a wooden spoon. Cook for 5 minutes on a low simmer to produce a lemon cream. Cool.

Beat the egg whites until soft peaks form, adding the remaining 1 cup (250 mL) of sugar halfway through. Continue whisking until the whites are firm and stand on their own. When the whites are firm, gently fold in the lemon cream.

Pour into the prepared soufflé dish and bake for 15 minutes. Serve immediately.

½ cup (125 mL) unsalted butter

1 cup (250 mL) freshly squeezed lemon juice (about 5 lemons)

2 cups (500 mL) sugar plus extra for sprinkling

12 large eggs, separated

Chef's tip | To maximize the amount of juice extracted from a lemon, roll the lemon on the counter back and forth for 30 seconds. You can also microwave the lemon for 20 seconds to release the juice.

Classic Cheesecake

SERVES: 12

Rich and creamy to please all palates! Decorate with fresh seasonal berries. For clean serving slices, run your knife under warm water between slices.

CRUST
1½ cups (375 mL) graham cracker crumbs

6 tablespoons (90 mL) unsalted butter, melted

¼ cup (60 mL) sugar

FILLING
1½ pounds (750 g) cream cheese, at room temperature

¾ cup (185 mL) sugar

1 teaspoon (5 mL) vanilla extract

3 large eggs, at room temperature

TOPPING
1 cup (250 mL) sour cream

¼ cup (60 mL) sugar

⅛ teaspoon (0.5 mL) salt

1 pint (500 mL) blueberries

Preheat oven to 350°F (180°C).

Lightly grease a 10-inch (25-cm) springform pan.

For the crust, combine the graham cracker crumbs, melted butter and sugar. Mix with a fork until moistened. Spread the mixture over the bottom of the pan and ½ inch (1 cm) up the sides, using your fingertips or the flat bottom of a drinking glass to press down on the crumbs.

Bake for 10–12 minutes, or until lightly browned and firm to the touch.

Remove from oven, and lower the oven temperature to 300°F (150°C).

For the filling, beat the cream cheese in the bowl of a stand mixer until light and creamy. Gradually add the sugar and vanilla. Beat in the eggs one at a time, scraping down the sides of the bowl after each addition.

Pour into the prepared crust and bake for 40–45 minutes just until the centre barely jiggles when the pan is tapped. Remove from the oven. Run a knife around the edges to release pressure from the sides so the cake does not crack in the middle. Cool on a rack for at least 1 hour.

For the topping, preheat oven to 425°F (220°C).

Combine the sour cream, sugar and salt, and spread over the cheesecake. Bake for 5 minutes. Cool completely on a rack.

Top with blueberries, or any other favourite berry, and refrigerate for at least 3 hours before serving.

Freezing: Freeze without the topping. Defrost cake in refrigerator and add topping before serving.

Chef's tip | DO NOT OVERBEAT THE FILLING OR IT WILL CAUSE THE CAKE TO CRACK.

Apple Crisp Cheesecake

SERVES: 8–10

Apples, cinnamon, brown sugar and cream—an easy to make cheesecake with great taste.

Preheat oven to 325°F (160°C).

Lightly grease a 10-inch (25-cm) round springform pan.

For the crust, combine the crumbs, oats, sugar and butter. Gently press into the pan.

For the topping, mix together the oats, sugar, flour, cinnamon and butter, and set aside.

For the filling, in a stand mixer, combine the cream cheese, sugar and sour cream. Blend eggs in one at a time. Blend in cinnamon and nutmeg. Pour into the crust. Arrange the apple slices decoratively on top.

Sprinkle the topping ingredients over the apples and bake for 65–75 minutes. The centre will still wiggle. The cake will continue to set in the pan.

Remove from the oven and run a knife around the sides of the pan to release the cake from the sides so it does not crack. Cool completely on a rack and refrigerate in the pan.

Remove from pan and serve.

CRUST
2 cups (500 mL) graham cracker or ginger snap crumbs

1 cup (250 mL) rolled oats

⅓ cup (75 mL) packed brown sugar

⅔ cup (150 mL) unsalted butter, melted

TOPPING
¼ cup (60 mL) rolled oats

¼ cup (60 mL) packed brown sugar

¼ cup (60 mL) all-purpose flour

1 teaspoon (5 mL) cinnamon

2 tablespoons (30 mL) unsalted butter

FILLING
1.5 pounds (750 g) cream cheese, at room temperature

1 cup (250 mL) packed brown sugar

¾ cup (185 mL) sour cream

4 large eggs

1¾ teaspoons (9 mL) cinnamon

½ teaspoon (2 mL) nutmeg

1 apple, peeled, cored and sliced

Tiramisu

An Italian trifle that is often made with stale sponge cake that is soaked in espresso and brandy. When translated literally, tiramisu means "pick me up"—and it certainly does! This version is made without eggs. For a sophisticated finale, prepare the tiramisu in individual martini glasses.

2 pounds (1 kg) mascarpone cheese, at room temperature

1½ cups (375 mL) heavy (35%) cream

1¼ cups (310 mL) sugar

2 teaspoons (10 mL) vanilla extract

2½ cups (625 mL) cold strong espresso coffee

¼ cup (60 mL) brandy or dark rum

1 14.10-ounce (400-g) package ladyfinger cookies (about 40 cookies)

¼ cup (60 mL) unsweetened cocoa powder

shaved semisweet chocolate, for garnish

This can be prepared either in a large trifle bowl or a 9 x 13-inch (3.5-L) dish.

In a large stand mixer bowl, beat the marscapone, cream, sugar and vanilla for 2 minutes until thick and creamy.

In a shallow bowl, mix the cold coffee with the brandy or rum. Lightly dip half the ladyfingers into the liquid one at a time and place them very close together in the trifle bowl or dish.

Spread half the mascarpone mixture over the soaked ladyfingers. Sift half the cocoa powder over the mascarpone through a fine mesh sieve. Top with the remaining ladyfingers, dipped in espresso mixture, then with the remaining mascarpone to make another layer. Sprinkle with the cocoa powder again.

Cover the dish with plastic wrap and refrigerate for several hours. The longer it rests, the more flavourful it will be. Just before serving, remove the plastic wrap and sprinkle some shaved chocolate overtop.

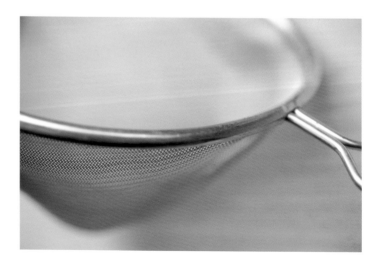

Crème Brûlée

D

SERVES: 8

The beauty of this classic French dessert is the juxtaposition of the soft and creamy custard tucked under a brittle sheet of caramelized brown sugar. If you prefer to omit the crust, this dessert can be served simply as pots de crème.

Preheat oven to 350°F (180°C).

In a double boiler, scald the cream (heat to just before boiling) over simmering water. Stir in the sugar and vanilla.

In a large bowl, whisk the yolks until frothy, around 3 minutes. Gradually pour the hot cream into the yolks, stirring constantly to make sure the eggs do not curdle. Strain into eight 4-ounce (125-mL) ramekins to eliminate any coagulated bits of eggs. Skim off any bubbles from the surface.

Place the ramekins in a large baking pan. Add enough hot water to the pan to come halfway up the sides of the cups and bake for 32–35 minutes until a skin forms on the surface. Remove the ramekins from the water with tongs and chill for 2 hours or overnight. Chilling is crucial to allow the custard to set.

Preheat broiler. Arrange rack 5 inches (12 cm) away from broiler.

Set the ramekins on a rimmed baking sheet. Sprinkle each custard with 1 tablespoon (15 mL) sugar, making sure there are no lumps. Broil until the sugar turns golden, about 2 minutes. Watch closely to avoid burning. Do not overcook or the custard will bubble through the sugar.

If you have a handheld blowtorch, torch the topping until it is brown and bubbling.

Cool. Serve within 2–3 hours so the caramel stays crisp.

---

3 cups (750 mL) whipping cream

6 tablespoons (90 mL) sugar

2 teaspoons (10 mL) vanilla extract

6 large egg yolks

½ cup (125 mL) packed brown sugar, for topping

Apple Custard Cake Parisienne

SERVES: 12

An impressive cake that raises the bar on sophistication. A wonderful dessert to serve for Rosh Hashanah when apples are celebrated and plentiful.

BASE

2 cups (500 mL) all-purpose flour

2 teaspoons (10 mL) baking powder

1 cup (250 mL) sugar

2 large eggs, at room temperature

½ cup (125 mL) unsalted butter or margarine, melted

4 pounds (2 kg) apples, peeled, cored and thinly sliced

CUSTARD

¼ cup (60 mL) unsalted butter or margarine, melted

1 cup (250 mL) sugar

1 large egg

1 teaspoon (5 mL) vanilla extract

Preheat oven to 350°F (180°C).

Lightly grease a 9-inch (1.5-L) springform pan.

For the base, in a medium-size bowl sift the flour and baking powder together. Set aside.

In a large bowl, beat the sugar and eggs together. Add the melted butter and stir. Stir in the sifted flour and baking powder. The batter should be thick and glossy. Spread the mixture with a spatula on the bottom and halfway up the sides of the springform pan.

Fill the prepared pan with apples right up to the top, arranging the top slices decoratively in concentric circles. Bake for 1 hour and 15 minutes. Cover lightly with aluminum foil if the apples get too dark.

For the custard, beat the butter, sugar, egg and vanilla together in a large bowl until well blended. Carefully pour the custard over the cake and continue to bake for another 20 minutes. Cool thoroughly and refrigerate overnight before serving.

Variation: Try using an assortment of apples to add interesting flavour and texture. Some choices are Braeburn, Golden Delicious, Granny Smith, Fuji and Northern Spy. Avoid McIntosh, Baldwin and Cortland because they do not hold their shape. ♦ Individual portions can be served with Caramel Sauce (see page 191).

Grilled Pineapple
with Caramel Sauce

SERVES: 6–8

𝒜 *wonderful backyard dessert that is simple yet delicious. Grilling draws out the natural sweetness of fruit. The caramel sauce can be prepared up to one week ahead and stored in the refrigerator until needed. Warm in the microwave before serving.*

Preheat grill to medium heat, or preheat the broiler.

For the pineapple, cut the tops and bottoms from the pineapples. Use a knife to peel the pineapples, cutting from top to bottom. Slice the fruit into ½-inch (1-cm) slices (rings), and use a cookie cutter to remove the firm inner core. Put the pineapple slices on the grill (or under the broiler), grilling for 3–4 minutes per side, turning once to achieve crosshatched grill marks.

For the caramel sauce, melt the sugar and water in a medium saucepan over medium-high heat. Bring to a boil. Cook, swirling the pan occasionally, until the mixture is amber brown and caramelized, about 7 minutes.

Remove the caramel from the heat and slowly add the heavy cream. Be careful because it will splash up when the cool liquid is added. It will also make the caramel harden—this is normal!

Stir over medium heat until the mixture is smooth. For a thinner caramel, add up to ½ cup (125 mL) of milk.

To serve, plate the pineapple and top with a scoop of ice cream and warm caramel sauce.

Variation: Substitute peaches or mangos for pineapple. ♦ Substitute soy milk for the cream (which will result in a thinner sauce).

Freezing: The caramel sauce can be frozen.

---

3 fresh pineapples, peeled and cut into ¾-inch (2-cm) slices

CARAMEL SAUCE
MAKES: ABOUT 1½ CUPS (375 mL)

1 cup (250 mL) sugar

¼ cup (60 mL) water

1 cup (250 mL) heavy (35%) cream

½ cup (125 mL) whole milk, optional

TO SERVE
2 pints (1 L) good quality vanilla ice cream

Rustic Plum Galette

MAKES: DOUGH FOR 2 GALETTES, EACH 11 INCHES (28 CM) IN DIAMETER

A freestyle tart that enfolds seasonal fruits with an almond filling. The country-styled pleated pastry crust comes out of the oven golden and crisp and tucks the juicy fruit inside. You can also use peaches, nectarines or pineapple slices. The frangipane can be kept, tightly covered, in the refrigerator for one to two days.

SWEET GALETTE DOUGH

2½ cups (375 mL) all-purpose flour

2 tablespoons (30 mL) sugar

½ teaspoon (2 mL) salt

1 cup (250 mL) unsalted butter, chilled and cut into ½-inch (1-cm) pieces

⅔ cup (150 mL) ice water

ALMOND FRANGIPANE FILLING
(ENOUGH FOR 1 GALETTE)

½ cup (5 oz / 150 g) packed almond paste

¼ cup (60 mL) sugar

¼ cup (60 mL) unsalted butter, at room temperature

1 tablespoon (15 mL) dark rum

1 large egg, at room temperature

TO ASSEMBLE

1 pound (500 g) (firm) plums

1 tablespoon (15 mL) unsalted butter, melted

2 teaspoons (10 mL) sugar

For the dough, mix together the flour, sugar and salt in a large food processor bowl. Add the butter. Mix until the butter is evenly distributed but still in fairly large visible pieces. Add all but 2 tablespoons (30 mL) of the ice water all at once to the flour and butter.

Mix the dough until it just begins to come together. Be cautious. Do not over-mix, just pulse! If it is too dry, add the reserved water gradually. Gather the dough with your hands; do not worry if you see streaks of butter. It will melt and help add flakiness to the dough.

Divide the dough in half. Shape into 2 disks. Wrap each disk separately in plastic and refrigerate for at least 1 hour before shaping.

For the filling, beat together the almond paste, sugar and butter with an electric mixer. Add the rum and egg and continue to mix until smooth.

Preheat oven to 400°F (200°C).

To assemble, cut each plum in half, remove the pit and cut the flesh into ¼-inch (5-mm) thick slices.

Line a 12 x 15-inch (30 x 38-cm) baking sheet, preferably without sides, with parchment paper.

On a lightly floured surface, roll 1 of the galette dough disks into a 15-inch (38-cm) round. Transfer the dough by folding it in half, picking it up and unfolding it on the prepared baking sheet.

Spread the frangipane over the dough, leaving a 2-inch (5-cm) border all around. Arrange the plum slices in an even layer over the frangipane. Lift the edges of the dough and fold them inward over the filling, pleating them to create an attractive folded-over border. Brush the border with melted butter and sprinkle the galette with sugar.

Bake until the crust has browned and the frangipane is set, about 30–35 minutes. Let cool for about 5 minutes and then slide the galette off the paper and onto a cooling rack. Cool for 20 minutes before slicing.

Variations: You can also divide the dough into 6 pieces to make individual galettes. Reduce the baking time to about 20 minutes. ◆ Double the frangipane recipe if preparing two galettes.

Freezing: The dough can be made ahead of time and frozen up to 1 month. Wrap in plastic wrap and thaw in the refrigerator.

Chef's tip | IF ALMOND PASTE DRIES OUT, DO NOT DISCARD. PLACE BLOCK IN A RESEALABLE BAG ALONG WITH A PIECE OF BREAD. THE MOISTURE FROM THE BREAD WILL RESTORE THE ALMOND PASTE TO A PLIABLE STATE.

Apple Berry Crisp
with Oatmeal Streusel Topping

SERVES: 6–8

Heartwarming and comforting, this baked dish can be prepared in a pinch with minimal effort. This warm fruit dish is perfect when served with ice cream.

FILLING

¾ cup (185 mL) sugar

¼ cup (60 mL) all-purpose or whole wheat flour

grated zest of 1 lemon

6–8 Golden Delicious apples, peeled and sliced (about 6 cups / 1.5 L)

2 cups (500 mL) assorted fresh or frozen unsweetened berries (blueberries, cranberries, raspberries)

STREUSEL TOPPING

1½ cups (375 mL) quick-cooking rolled oats

¾ cup (185 mL) packed brown sugar

¼ cup (60 mL) all-purpose flour

2 teaspoons (10 mL) cinnamon

6 tablespoons (90 mL) melted butter or margarine

Preheat oven to 375°F (190°C).

Grease a 13 x 9-inch (3.5-L) baking dish.

For the filling, stir together the sugar, flour and lemon zest in a large bowl. Add the apples and the berries. Stir gently to mix. Pour into the baking dish.

For the streusel topping, stir together the oats, sugar, flour and cinnamon in a small bowl. Pour the butter over the oat mixture and toss to mix. The mixture should be a bit clumpy. Sprinkle the mixture over the fruit and bake for 40–50 minutes until the topping is golden and the apples are bubbling and tender.

Serve warm.

Variation: Experiment with peaches or nectarines instead of the apples. You can also use dried berries instead of fresh, but decrease the sugar to taste because dried fruit is very sweet.

Chef's tip | YOU DO NOT NEED TO DEFROST THE BERRIES BEFORE USING. ADD THEM DIRECTLY TO THE BATTER.

Flourless Chocolate Torte

F D

SERVES: 10

*S*erve a wedge of this rich dense torte on a pool of Raspberry Coulis (see page 208). Scatter fresh berries around the plate. The torte can be served at Passover.

Preheat oven to 325°F (160°C).

Lightly grease an 8-inch (20-cm) springform pan and line it with parchment paper.

Melt the chocolate, butter or margarine and coffee or liqueur in a double boiler over simmering water. Remove from heat and cool to lukewarm.

In a stand mixer, beat the eggs until doubled in volume, at least 5 minutes. The mixture will be thick and fluffy.

Gently fold the eggs into the chocolate mixture. Do not overbeat. Pour into the springform pan and bake for 35–40 minutes.

Remove the cake from the oven. The centre will wobble when the pan is moved, but the sides will be firm. Cool. The cake will have puffed up in the oven and will deflate as it cools.

1 pound (500 g) bittersweet
or semi-sweet chocolate, chopped

1 cup (250 mL) unsalted butter
or margarine

2 tablespoons (30 mL) strong coffee
or rum

8 large eggs, at room temperature

Chef's tips | STORE CHOCOLATE IN A COOL, DRY PLACE IN A SEALED PACKAGE SO THAT IT WILL NOT ABSORB ODOURS.

FAT "BLOOMING," THE WHITISH COATING YOU SOMETIMES SEE ON CHOCOLATE, OCCURS IN CHOCOLATE THAT HAS BEEN EXPOSED TO SIGNIFICANT CHANGES IN TEMPERATURE. IT IS STILL PERFECT FOR BAKING BUT A LITTLE LESS PRETTY.

Molten Chocolate Cakes

SERVES: 10

These individual cakes are slightly underbaked so that the chocolate centre oozes out when cut. To maximize flavour and depth use good quality chocolate with a high cocoa content. The batter can be made one day ahead and kept covered and chilled until needed.

10 ounces (300 g) bittersweet (not unsweetened) or semisweet chocolate, chopped

10 tablespoons (150 mL) unsalted butter or margarine

4 large eggs

4 large egg yolks

pinch of salt

1 cup (250 mL) sugar

½ cup (125 mL) all-purpose flour

fresh berries, optional

fresh mint leaves, optional

vanilla ice cream, optional

Preheat oven to 400°F (200°C).

Butter 10 ¾-cup (185-mL) ramekins or custard cups.

Stir the chocolate and butter together in a heavy medium-size saucepan over low heat until melted. Cool to lukewarm.

Whisk the eggs, egg yolks and salt in a stand mixer to blend. Whisk in the sugar and beat until the batter falls in a heavy ribbon when the beaters are lifted, about 6 minutes. Sift the flour over the egg mixture and mix. Gradually fold in the lukewarm chocolate mixture.

Divide the batter equally among the 10 ramekins. Place the ramekins on a baking sheet. Bake until the sides of the cakes are set and the centre begins to crack but remains soft, about 16–18 minutes. Run a small knife around the cakes to loosen them. Immediately turn the cakes out onto plates.

Sprinkle with berries and fresh mint leaves and serve with ice cream.

Freezing: The batter can be frozen in ramekins for up to 1 week. Bake for 19 minutes from frozen.

Chef's tips | TO PREPARE THE ICE CREAM SCOOPS IN ADVANCE, SCOOP THE ICE CREAM ONTO A BAKING SHEET. FREEZE FOR 30 MINUTES. PLACE IN A RESEALABLE BAG OR BOWL IN THE FREEZER UNTIL READY TO USE.

ALWAYS SEPARATE EGGS WHEN COLD. FOR GREATER VOLUME, BEAT THEM AT ROOM TEMPERATURE. FREEZE LEFTOVER EGG WHITES IN AN ICE CUBE TRAY, 1 PER COMPARTMENT, THEN POP THEM OUT AND STORE IN A PLASTIC RESEALABLE BAG. THAW IN THE REFRIGERATOR BEFORE USING.

Flourless Chocolate-Orange Almond Cake

SERVES: 8–10

*C*hocolate and orange have an affinity for one another and this dessert certainly attests to it. This cake is a perfect Passover treat that is rich in flavour.

Preheat oven to 350°F (180°C).

Generously grease the bottom of a 10-inch (25-cm) springform pan.

Blend the almonds and ¼ cup (60 mL) of the sugar in a food processor until the almonds are finely ground. Add the chocolate and pulse until the chocolate is finely ground, scraping the sides and bottom of the bowl occasionally.

In a small bowl, whisk together the cocoa powder, orange juice and orange zest until smooth.

Combine the egg yolks and ½ cup (125 mL) plus 2 tablespoons (30 mL) of sugar in a large bowl. Scrape in the seeds from the vanilla bean. Discard bean. Use an electric mixer to beat the yolk mixture until it is very thick, about 4 minutes. Beat in the cocoa mixture, then fold in the ground almond mixture.

Using clean dry beaters, beat the egg whites and salt in another large bowl until soft peaks form. Gradually add 2 tablespoons (30 mL) of remaining sugar, beating until the whites are stiff but not dry. Fold the whites into the chocolate batter in 3 additions. Transfer to the prepared pan.

Bake the cake for about 40 minutes, until a wooden pick inserted into the centre comes out clean. Cool the cake completely in the pan on a rack. Cut around the edges of the cake then release the sides of the pan. Cut cake into wedges and transfer to plates for serving.

Variation: Substitute 1 teaspoon (5 mL) vanilla extract for the vanilla bean.

1¼ cups (310 mL) whole almonds (6–7 ounces / 175–225 g)

1 cup (250 mL) sugar, divided

6 ounces (170 g) bittersweet (not unsweetened) or semisweet chocolate, coarsely chopped

½ cup (125 mL) unsweetened cocoa powder

½ cup (125 mL) orange juice

2 teaspoons (10 mL) grated orange zest

6 large eggs, separated

1 vanilla bean, split lengthwise

¼ teaspoon (1 mL) salt

Kentucky Pecan Pie

SERVES: 8

𝒜 quick and easy pie that will transport the flavour of the south into your home. Serve with a dollop of bourbon whipped cream or ice cream. You can whip the bourbon cream up to 1 hour in advance, and refrigerate until ready to serve.

1 9-inch (23-cm) unbaked pie shell

FILLING
1 cup (250 mL) light corn syrup

1 cup (250 mL) packed dark brown sugar

⅓ teaspoon (1 mL) salt

⅓ cup (75 mL) melted unsalted butter or margarine

1 teaspoon (5 mL) vanilla extract or dark rum

3 large eggs, slightly beaten

1 heaping cup (250 mL) pecans, toasted

¼ cup (60 mL) semisweet chocolate chips, optional

BOURBON WHIPPED CREAM
MAKES: 2–2½ CUPS (500–625 mL)

1 cup (250 mL) whipping or heavy (35%) cream, chilled

2 tablespoons (30 mL) sugar

1 tablespoon (15 mL) bourbon or ½ teaspoon (2.5 mL) cinnamon

Preheat oven to 350°F (180°C).

Transfer the pie shell to a 9-inch (23-cm) dish. If the shell cracks or breaks in the process, simply pinch it back together.

For the filling, combine the syrup, sugar, salt, butter or margarine and vanilla extract in a bowl and mix well. Add the slightly beaten eggs. Pour this mixture into the unbaked pie shell. Sprinkle over the pecans and chocolate chips, if using, or make a pattern with the pecans.

Bake for 45 minutes to 1 hour, or until the filling is set. Cover the crust of the pie with aluminum foil if it starts to burn. Do not overbake the pie or the filling will be tough. Cool on a baking rack before serving.

For the bourbon whipped cream, in a chilled bowl of a stand mixer, whisk the cream, sugar and bourbon or cinnamon until stiff peaks form. Be careful not to overwhip the cream because it will turn into butter.

Variations: To add more creaminess and richness to the filling, add ½ cup (125 mL) of heavy (35%) cream into the corn syrup mixture. ♦ You can use the galette dough (see page 192) instead of a store-bought pie shell.

Chef's tip | TO RESCUE CREAM THAT YOU'VE OVERWHIPPED, GENTLY FOLD IN A FEW TABLESPOONS OF MILK OR UNWHIPPED CREAM.

Citrus Pound Cake

MAKES: 1 BUNDT OR 1 TUBE CAKE, OR 2 (9 x 5-INCH / 2-L) LOAVES

A perfect picnic cake that slices beautifully. To ensure success, have all the ingredients at room temperature.

Preheat oven to 350°F (180°C).

Grease and flour a 10-inch (25-cm) tube or Bundt pan or two 9 x 5-inch (2-L) loaf pans.

For the cake, combine the flour, baking powder, baking soda and salt. Set aside.

Cream the butter with the sugar on medium speed in a stand mixer until well blended. Add the eggs, one at a time, beating lightly after each addition until smooth, then beat on high speed until thick and creamy, about 5 minutes. Add the zests and blend.

Mix the yogurt and orange juice together in a bowl.

Add the dry ingredients alternately with the yogurt and orange juice mixture to the butter mixture, ending with the dry ingredients, and beating on low speed until blended. Make sure to scrape down the sides of the bowl.

Spread the batter in the prepared pan and bake about 65 minutes (55 minutes if using loaf pans) or until a wooden pick inserted in the centre of the cake comes out clean. Even if the centre bounces back, make sure the pick is clean to avoid having patches of gumminess in the cake. Cool for 10 minutes in the pan, then remove to a baking rack.

For the syrup, heat the sugar and juice together, stirring to dissolve the sugar.

Use a toothpick to poke holes in the surface of the warm cake. Brush the syrup over the cake with a pastry brush, allowing the syrup to penetrate. Cool cake completely before slicing.

Variation: Dust the cake with confectioners' sugar for a quick finish.

CAKE
3 cups (750 mL) all-purpose flour

½ teaspoon (2 mL) baking powder

½ teaspoon (2 mL) baking soda

¾ teaspoon (4 mL) salt

1 cup (250 mL) unsalted butter, at room temperature

2¼ cups (560 mL) sugar

4 large eggs, at room temperature

1 tablespoon (15 mL) freshly grated orange zest

2 teaspoons (10 mL) freshly grated lemon zest

¾ cup (185 mL) 2% or non-fat plain yogurt, at room temperature

⅓ cup (75 mL) orange juice

LEMON SYRUP
⅓ cup (75 mL) sugar

¼ cup (60 mL) fresh lemon juice

Whisky Honey Cake

Makes: 1 Bundt cake or 2 9 x 5-inch (2-L) loaves

Nothing welcomes a new year better than a homemade honey loaf. You can divide the batter among small loaf pans and give the loaves as holiday gifts. Sprinkle with sifted confectioners' sugar for an attractive garnish.

4 large eggs

1 cup (250 mL) sugar

¾ cup (185 mL) oil

1½ cups (375 mL) liquid honey

¾ cup (185 mL) cold coffee or tea

¼ cup (60 mL) whisky or rum

3 cups (750 mL) all-purpose flour

1 tablespoon (15 mL) baking powder

½ teaspoon (2 mL) baking soda

1 teaspoon (5 mL) cinnamon

½ teaspoon (2 mL) allspice

¼ teaspoon (1 mL) grated nutmeg

½ cup (125 mL) chopped pecans, toasted, optional

½ cup (125 mL) raisins, optional

Preheat oven to 350°F (180°C).

In a large bowl, beat the eggs and sugar together. Add the oil and honey.

In a small bowl, combine the coffee or tea and liquor. In another bowl, mix the flour, baking powder, baking soda and spices. Mix the dry ingredients into the egg mixture alternately with the coffee or tea mixture until all the dry ingredients are incorporated. Stir in the pecans and raisins, if using.

Pour into an ungreased 10-inch (25-cm) tube pan or Bundt pan or two 9 x 5-inch (2-L) loaf pans. Bake for about 15 minutes. Reduce the heat to 300°F (150°C) and bake for a further hour. Remove from oven and cool for 15 minutes on a baking rack before inverting onto a plate.

Chef's tips | WHEN MEASURING HONEY, ALWAYS LIGHTLY GREASE YOUR MEASURING CUP FIRST SO THE HONEY COMES OUT SMOOTHLY AND YOU DO NOT LOSE A LOT OF THE MEASURED AMOUNT.

IF HONEY SOLIDIFIES, PLACE IN THE MICROWAVE FOR 10 SECONDS TO LIQUEFY.

Passover Apple Cake

SERVES: 12

An attractive dessert that can be presented family style or individually plated for the Seder.

Preheat oven to 350°F (180°C).

Grease a 9 x 13-inch (3.5-L) baking pan.

Combine the apples, sugar, cinnamon and nuts, if using, and set aside.

For the batter, combine the eggs, sugar, oil, lemon juice, zest and salt in a mixer on low speed. Sift together the potato starch and cake meal and add slowly to the egg mixture.

For the topping, combine the sugar, cinnamon and nuts, if using, and set aside.

To assemble the cake, spread half the batter over the bottom of the pan. Add the apple filling, then pour the remaining batter over the apples. Sprinkle the topping over the top layer of batter.

Bake for 45 minutes, then reduce the oven temperature to 325°F (160°C) and bake for a further 30–45 minutes or until golden.

Chef's tip | MATZO CAKE MEAL IS A FINER GRANULATION OF MATZO MEAL. IT WORKS BEST IN COMBINATION WITH POTATO STARCH. POTATO STARCH ADDS TENDERNESS TO BAKED GOODS.

FILLING
6 large apples, peeled and coarsely grated

2 tablespoons (30 mL) sugar

1–2 teaspoons (5–10 mL) cinnamon

3 tablespoons (45 mL) ground pecans or walnuts, optional

BATTER
6 large eggs

1½ cups (375 mL) sugar

1 cup (250 mL) vegetable oil

1 tablespoon (15 mL) fresh lemon juice

1 teaspoon (5 mL) grated lemon zest

dash of salt

¾ cup (185 mL) potato starch

1½ cups (375 mL) matzo cake meal

TOPPING
½ cup (125 mL) sugar

2 teaspoons (10 mL) cinnamon

¼ cup (60 mL) chopped pecans or walnuts, optional

Passover Lemon Meringue Freeze

SERVES: 6–8

A refreshing lemon dessert that is an outstanding finale to a Seder meal. The pie filling must be frozen overnight before completing the recipe.

FILLING

3 large eggs

3 large egg yolks

½ cup (125 mL) freshly squeezed lemon juice

½ teaspoon (2 mL) freshly grated lemon zest

1¼ cups (310 mL) plus 1 tablespoon (15 mL) sugar

4 large egg whites, at room temperature

CRUST

2 packages Passover mandlebread or about ½ pound (250 g) homemade

3 tablespoons (45 mL) melted unsalted butter or margarine

MERINGUE TOPPING

6 large egg whites

1 tablespoon (15 mL) sugar

For the filling, combine the 3 whole eggs with the egg yolks, lemon juice, zest and 1¼ cups (310 mL) of the sugar in a double boiler. Heat and stir until thickened, about 10 minutes. It will look like pudding. Cool.

In a stand mixer, beat the 4 egg whites with 1 tablespoon (15 mL) of sugar until stiff. Fold into the cooled lemon mixture.

Butter a 9-inch (23-cm) springform pan.

For the crust, grind the mandlebread in the food processor, then add the butter or margarine. Pat into the bottom of the prepared pan.

To assemble, pour lemon filling evenly over the crust. Freeze overnight.

To prepare the meringue, beat the 6 egg whites until foamy. Gradually add the sugar and continue to beat until stiff peaks form. Spread over the lemon filling. Spread right to the sides because the filling shrinks. Use the back of a teaspoon to create attractive peaks.

Preheat the broiler.

Place under the broiler until the meringue is lightly browned, only a couple of minutes. Watch carefully, the meringue can go from lightly browned to burnt in seconds. Cool for 2 minutes and return to the freezer.

Remove from the freezer 15 minutes before serving. Remove sides of pan.

Chef's tip | TO FREEZE EGG YOLKS, BEAT INTO EVERY ¼ CUP (60 mL) EGG YOLKS (4 YOLKS) EITHER ⅛ TEASPOON (0.5 mL) SALT OR 1½ TEASPOONS (7 mL) SUGAR. LABEL THE CONTAINER WITH THE NUMBER OF YOLKS, THE DATE AND WHETHER YOU HAVE ADDED SALT (SAVOURY) OR SUGAR (SWEET).

Poached Pears

SERVES: 4–6

An elegant and tasty dessert. Poaching fruit is a simple technique that transforms ordinary fruit into dessert show pieces. Serve with Chocolate Fudge Sauce (see page 207) or Raspberry Coulis (see page 208).

Peel and halve the pears, leaving the stems intact, and scoop out the inside cavity of the pear with a melon baller, removing the entire core and all the seeds. Place the pears as you peel them in the 3 cups (750 mL) of water with the lemon juice to prevent browning.

In a stockpot, heat the apple juice or cider, sugar and spices. Bring to a boil, then add the pears. Keep at a low simmer. Turn the pears with a wooden spoon every 10 minutes to make sure they are cooked evenly.

After 20 minutes, prick the pears with the tip of a paring knife. If it slides through easily, they are ready. The poaching time will vary, depending on the size and ripeness of the pear.

Remove the pears from the pot and continue cooking the juices on high heat to reduce to about 1 cup (250 mL). Place the pears back in the pot to absorb the flavours and warm through.

Serve warm or at room temperature.

Variation: Try a vanilla bean or lemongrass instead of cinnamon for a tasty change.

Chef's tip | IF YOU DO NOT HAVE APPLE JUICE OR CIDER, YOU CAN USE DRY RED OR WHITE WINE, OR EVEN STEEPED TEA. NOTE THAT THE PEARS WILL CHANGE COLOUR DEPENDING ON THE TYPE OF LIQUID USED.

4–6 large firm Bosc pears, with stems

3 cups (750 mL) cold water

juice of 1 lemon

2 cups (500 mL) unsweetened apple juice or cider

1 cup (250 mL) sugar

1 cinnamon stick

6 peppercorns

Peach and Raspberry Ice Cream Cake with Meringue Topping

FD

SERVES: 10–12

Do not be intimidated by the prospect of making meringue. In this recipe it is browned under the broiler, like a baked Alaska, for a dramatic effect. The cake can be made two days ahead. Cover and keep frozen.

CRUST
3 cups (750 mL) graham cracker crumbs

¾ cup (185 mL) confectioners' sugar

¾ cup (185 mL) unsalted butter, melted

FILLING
1 pint (500 mL) peach ice cream or frozen yogurt

1 pint (500 mL) raspberry sorbet

1 pint (500 mL) good quality vanilla ice cream

MERINGUE
4 large egg whites

¼ teaspoon (1 mL) cream of tartar

pinch of salt

½ cup (125 mL) sugar

¾ teaspoon (4 mL) vanilla extract

Preheat oven to 350°F (180°C).

Butter a 9-inch (23-cm) diameter springform pan with 2¾-inch (7-cm) sides.

For the crust, blend the crumbs and sugar in the food processor. Add the melted butter and process until the crumbs are evenly moistened. Gently press the crumb mixture over the bottom and up the sides of the pan. Bake the crust until slightly crisp, about 12 minutes. Cool crust completely, then freeze for 15 minutes.

For the filling, microwave the peach ice cream on low for three 10-second intervals until slightly softened. Drop the ice cream by large spoonfuls over the bottom of the crust, then spread over the crust. Place the pan in the freezer for 15 minutes.

Microwave the raspberry sorbet on low for three 10-second intervals until slightly softened. Spoon the sorbet in large dollops over the peach ice cream, then spread in an even layer. Return the pan to the freezer for 15 minutes.

Repeat with the vanilla ice cream, making sure it is spread smoothly. Freeze until the filling is firm, about 4 hours.

For the meringue, use an electric mixer to beat the egg whites in a large bowl until foamy. Add the cream of tartar and salt, and beat until soft peaks form. Gradually add the sugar and beat until the meringue is stiff and glossy, about 5 minutes. Beat in the vanilla.

Spoon the meringue over the cake, mounding in the centre and spreading right to the edge of the pan. Using a rubber spatula or knife, swirl the meringue decoratively, creating pointy tips. Freeze for 2 hours before serving.

Preheat broiler.

Broil cake just until the meringue begins to turn light golden, about 2 minutes. Carefully remove the pan sides and place the cake on a platter. Serve within 10 minutes.

Freezing: You can also prepare the meringue in advance and freeze the whole cake. Remove from the freezer 15 minutes before serving to soften.

Chef's tips | WHEN SEPARATING EGGS INTO YOLKS AND WHITES, IT IS *VERY* IMPORTANT TO NOT GET ANY YOLK IN THE WHITES BECAUSE THE FAT IN THE YOLK WILL PREVENT THE WHITES FROM INCREASING IN VOLUME. IT IS ESSENTIAL THAT THE BEATERS AND BOWL ARE SPOTLESS AND FREE OF ANY FAT.

ICE CREAM, FROZEN YOGURT OR SORBET CAN BE THAWED ON THE COUNTERTOP.

⒡ ⒫

Homemade Chunky Applesauce

SERVES: 4–6

𝒜 wonderful way to use up the apples your kids picked on their day trip to the orchard. An easy, wonderful dessert or snack on its own or as a topping to lacy latkes. To add some colour to the sauce, keep some of the skins on the apples. This keeps refrigerated for up to one week.

2 pounds (1 kg) apples (Macintosh, Pippin, Granny Smith), peeled, cored and cut into ½-inch (1-cm) slices

juice of 1 lemon

2 2-inch (5-cm) cinnamon sticks

3–4 tablespoons (45–60 mL) sugar

Place the apples, lemon juice and cinnamon sticks in a large pot on medium-high heat. Cover and bring to a boil. Reduce to a simmer and cook for 15 minutes. Add sugar to taste.

Remove the cover and stir, breaking up the softened apples. Continue to simmer and stir until the sauce has reached the desired texture. For a smoother texture, remove cinnamon sticks and run the cooled applesauce through a food mill or food processor.

Chocolate Fudge Sauce

D

MAKES: 3 CUPS (750 ML)

A decadent sauce that can dress up just about anything! Make sure to let it cool to thicken.

Bring the cream and corn syrup to a simmer in a large saucepan. Remove from the heat.

Add the chocolate and stir until melted and the mixture is smooth.

Let stand until slightly cooled and thickened, about 20 minutes.

This can be made 3 days ahead. Cover and chill until needed. Stir over low heat until just warm before serving.

1½ cups (375 mL) whipping cream

¼ cup (60 mL) dark corn syrup

1 pound (500 g) good quality bittersweet (not unsweetened) or semisweet chocolate, chopped

Chef's tip | WHEN CHOPPING CHOCOLATE, START AT ONE CORNER AND ALWAYS CHOP ON AN ANGLE. TRY TO CUT UNIFORM PIECES TO ENSURE EVEN MELTING.

Raspberry Coulis

F P

MAKES: ½ CUP (125 mL)

This uncooked, tart flavourful sauce will accent your dessert and temper excessive sweetness. A coulis is a purée or sauce.

1 cup (250 mL) unsweetened raspberries (fresh or frozen)
¼–½ cup (60–125 mL) sugar
1 teaspoon (5 mL) fresh lemon juice

Wash or thaw the raspberries as appropriate. Place them in a food processor or blender and purée. Continue processing and add ¼ cup (60 mL) sugar and lemon juice through the feed tube. Add more sugar as required.

Force the raspberry mixture through a fine mesh strainer with the back of a spoon to remove the seeds. Rub out all the seeds with a spatula.

Transfer the coulis into a squirt bottle for easy decorating or spoon onto your serving plates.

Variation: Experiment with other fruits like mango and strawberries.

Freezing: Freezes indefinitely.

Chef's tips | FRESH MINT LEAF IS A BEAUTIFUL ACCENT TO THE RED BERRIES AND MAKES A WONDERFUL GARNISH.

WHEN BERRIES ARE IN SEASON, MAKE A LOT OF COULIS AND FREEZE FOR LATER USE.

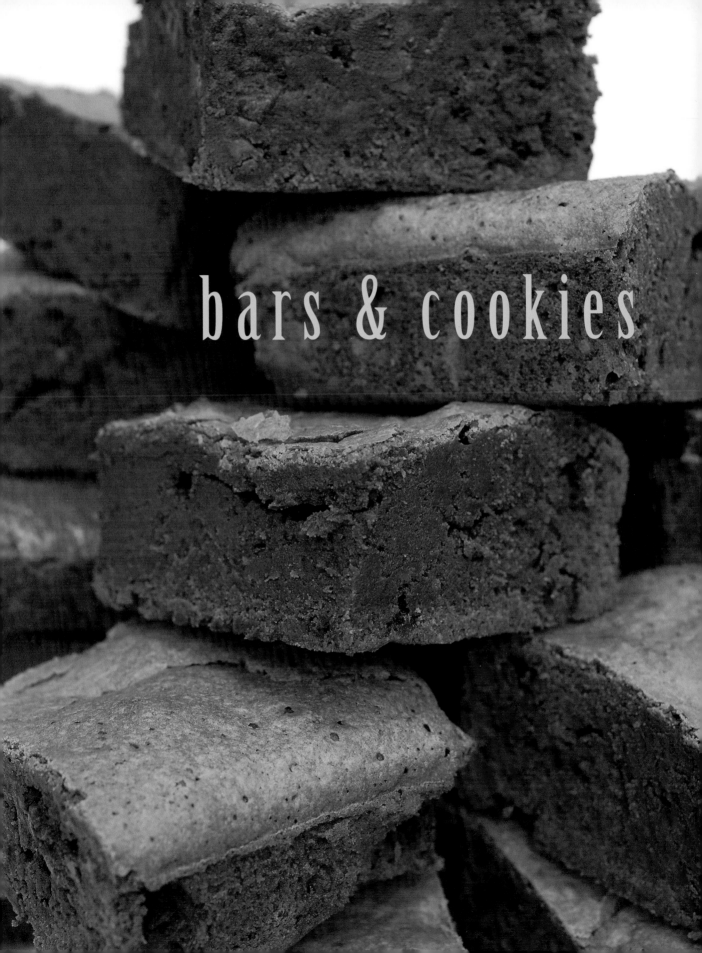

bars & cookies

Previous page: Triple Chocolate Fudge Brownies

Cranberry Pistachio Crisps

MAKES: ABOUT 2 DOZEN

These are so addictive! Sliced thinly, these cookies are light and crispy and make a great snack.

Preheat oven to 350°F (180°C).

Lightly grease a 9 x 5-inch (2-L) loaf pan.

Beat the eggs in a large bowl. Add the sugar and vanilla and beat until smooth. Add the flour, salt, nuts, dried fruit and zest. Mix together then pour the batter into the prepared pan.

Bake for 50–60 minutes, until golden brown. Cool. Remove from the pan, wrap in aluminum foil and refrigerate overnight.

Preheat oven to 350°F (180°C).

Line a baking sheet with parchment paper.

Place the chilled loaf on a cutting board. With a sharp knife, cut the loaf into fine slices, about ¼ inch (5 mm) thick, and place them on the baking sheet. Sprinkle with cinnamon sugar and bake for 10–15 minutes until golden and crispy. Cool.

Cookies can be stored in an airtight container or frozen.

4 large eggs, less one yolk
¾ cup (185 mL) sugar
½ teaspoon (2 mL) vanilla extract
1½ cups (375 mL) all-purpose flour
pinch salt
1 cup (250 mL) blanched whole almonds
¾ cup (185 mL) pistachio nuts
¾ cup (185 mL) dried cranberries
½ cup (125 mL) chopped dried apricots
freshly grated zest of 1 orange
1 tablespoon (15 mL) cinnamon sugar (see Chef's tip on page 222)

Ginger Cookies

MAKES: 2 DOZEN

A simple crackle cookie that smells heavenly and is nice with a cup of tea. Add some chopped crystallized ginger to the batter for a more intense ginger flavour.

⅔ cup (150 mL) canola oil

¾ cup (185 mL) sugar

1 large egg

¼ cup (60 mL) honey

2 cups (500 mL) all-purpose flour

2 teaspoons (10 mL) baking soda

2 teaspoon (10 mL) powdered ginger

pinch salt

2 tablespoons (30 mL) coarse white or brown sugar

Preheat oven to 350°F (180°C).

Line 2 baking sheets with parchment paper.

In a stand mixer, beat the oil and sugar together. Add the egg and honey and continue to beat.

In a separate bowl, mix together the flour, baking soda, ginger and salt. Add the dry ingredients into the egg mixture and mix until well combined. The dough will be soft and smooth.

Roll the dough into balls about 1 tablespoon (15 mL) in size. Place 2 inches (5 cm) apart on the baking sheet and press down with the back of an oiled spoon to flatten. Sprinkle with coarse sugar.

Bake for about 10–12 minutes or until lightly golden. The cookies will puff up and spread. Remove from baking sheet and cool on a wire rack.

Almond Crunch Biscotti

(F)(P)

MAKES: ABOUT 35 COOKIES

A twice-baked almond cookie, otherwise known as mandlebread. To serve, the cookies can be sprinkled with sifted confectioners' sugar and layered.

Preheat oven to 350°F (180°C).

Line a baking sheet with parchment paper.

In a mixing bowl, whisk together the oil and sugar. Add the eggs one at a time, making sure to incorporate all the ingredients. Stir in the vanilla extract.

In another bowl, mix together the flour, baking powder and salt. Add the dry ingredients into the wet. When the flour is just beginning to disappear, add the coconut, almonds, cereal, and chocolate. The batter will be lumpy but not sticky.

Divide the dough in two and shape it into two long logs. It does not matter what size you choose, but they must be equal so they will cook evenly. Keep wetting your hands to avoid sticking. Bake for about 30 minutes or until lightly browned and solid. Remove from oven.

Lower oven temperature to 300°F (150°C).

Cool the logs for 10 minutes and slice into 1-inch (2.5-cm) pieces. Turn the cookies on their sides and bake for another 10 minutes on each side to crisp. Cool and store in an airtight container.

Variation: Pecans or pistachios can be substituted for almonds.

¾ cup (185 mL) canola oil

1 cup (250 mL) sugar

2 large eggs

2 teaspoons (30 mL) vanilla extract

2 cups (500 mL) all-purpose flour

2 teaspoons (30 mL) baking powder

pinch salt

¼ cup (60 mL) grated unsweetened coconut

½ cup (125 mL) toasted slivered almonds

1 cup (250 mL) Grape-Nuts cereal

½ cup (125 mL) mini semisweet chocolate chips or chopped semisweet chocolate

Oatmeal Raisin Cookies

ⒻⒹ

MAKES: 48 COOKIES

These cookies spread when baked and are thin and chewy. Do not overbake unless you prefer crunchy cookies. Chocolate lovers can also add chocolate chips.

2 cups (500 mL) unsalted butter, at room temperature

2 cups (500 mL) sugar

1 cup (250 mL) packed brown sugar

2 teaspoons (10 mL) vanilla extract

2 large eggs

3 cups (750 mL) all-purpose flour

2 teaspoons (10 mL) baking soda

2 teaspoons (10 mL) cinnamon

3 cups (750 mL) rolled oats

2 cups (500 mL) raisins

2 cups (500 mL) pecan halves, optional

Preheat oven to 350°F (180°C).

Line 2 baking sheets with parchment paper.

Cream together the butter, sugars and vanilla. Add the eggs, one at a time.

Sift the flour, baking soda and cinammon. Add the dry ingredients to the egg mixture and mix until a dough forms. Stir in the oats, raisins and pecans, if using.

Roll the dough into balls, or use a mini ice cream scoop to make evenly sized balls. Place the balls 2 inches (5 cm) apart because they will spread. Bake for about 12–14 minutes, or until lightly golden.

Freezing: Freeze dough for up to 3 months in unbaked balls and bake from frozen as needed.

Chef's tip | ALWAYS BAKE COOKIES ON COOKIE SHEETS LINED WITH SILPAT MATS OR PARCHMENT PAPER. THERE IS NO NEED TO GREASE THE SHEETS, AND THE COOKIES JUST SLIDE RIGHT OFF.

Zesty Lemon Squares

F D

MAKES: 20 SQUARES

A colourful and fragrant addition to any sweet table. The freshly grated lemon zest complements the sweetness of the custard filling.

Preheat oven to 325°F (160°C).

Lightly grease and line a 9 x 13-inch (3.5-L) baking pan with parchment paper.

For the base, in the bowl of a stand mixer, combine the flour and confectioners' sugar. Using the paddle attachment, mix in the butter on low speed until the mixture is the size of small peas. Press into the bottom of the pan.

Bake for 20–25 minutes or until golden brown. Remove from oven. Lower the oven temperature to 300°F (150°C).

For the filling, in a large bowl whisk together the eggs and sugar until smooth. Stir in the lemon juice and zest, and then the flour.

Pour the lemon filling on top of the crust. Bake for about 35–40 minutes, until the lemon filling is set. Allow to cool on a cooling rack for half an hour. Cut into squares and dust with the ¼ cup (60 mL) of sifted confectioners' sugar.

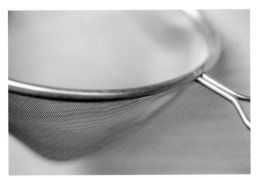

Chef's tip | ALWAYS SIFT CONFECTIONERS' SUGAR TO REMOVE LUMPS.

BASE
2 cups (500 mL) all-purpose flour

½ cup (125 mL) confectioners' sugar, sifted

½ cup (125 mL) cold unsalted butter or margarine

FILLING
6 large eggs

3 cups (750 mL) sugar

1 cup (250 mL) plus 2 tablespoons (30 mL) freshly squeezed lemon juice (4–5 lemons)

1 tablespoon (15 mL) freshly grated lemon zest

½ cup (125 mL) all-purpose flour

¼ cup (60 mL) confectioners' sugar for dusting

Triple Chocolate Fudge Brownies

FD

MAKES: 16 BROWNIES

Decadent and rich. These are always a big hit and can be prepared in minutes! To prepare for Passover, substitute 1 scant cup (250 mL) matzo cake meal (see Chef's tip on page 201) for the flour.

6 ounces (175 g) semisweet chocolate, chopped

2 ounces (50 g) unsweetened chocolate, chopped

¾ cup (185 mL) unsalted butter or margarine

4 large eggs, at room temperature

1½ cups (375 mL) sugar

1 teaspoon (5 mL) vanilla extract

1 cup (250 mL) all-purpose flour

½ teaspoon (2 mL) salt

1 cup (250 mL) semisweet chocolate chips

Preheat oven to 350°F (180°C).

Lightly grease an 8 x 8-inch (2-L) metal pan and line with parchment paper.

Melt the chopped chocolate with the butter either in the microwave or in the top of a double boiler. Cool to lukewarm.

In a large bowl, beat the eggs with the sugar until thick and fluffy, about 4 minutes. Add the vanilla and beat to combine. Mix in the chocolate mixture. Fold in the flour and salt to blend.

Add the chocolate chips and pour into the prepared baking dish.

Bake for 27–30 minutes or until set. It will start to crackle on top. Cool on a baking rack before cutting.

Variation: If you prefer a denser brownie, do not beat the eggs and sugar for as long.

Chef's tips | UNSWEETENED CHOCOLATE AND BITTER CHOCOLATE ARE BOTH MADE WITH 100 PERCENT COCOA LIQUOR. THEY ARE VERY BITTER AND ARE NOT INTENDED TO BE EATEN OUT OF THE WRAPPER!

SEMISWEET CHOCOLATE IS SIMILAR TO BITTER CHOCOLATE BUT CONTAINS LESS COCOA LIQUOR.

Chocolate Mint Bars

MAKES: 20 SQUARES

Sweet and refreshingly minty—an old-fashioned iced brownie that is a perfect finale to any dinner.

Preheat oven to 350°F (180°C).

Lightly grease and line an 8 x 8-inch (2-L) square pan with parchment paper.

For the base, in a microwave or in a double boiler, melt the chocolate with the butter. Stir in the sugar, eggs and peppermint extract. Add the flour and salt and mix well. Transfer into the prepared pan and bake for 25 minutes until set.

Cool on a rack.

For the filling, cream the butter, sugar and cream by hand until smooth.

Spread the mixture over the cooled base and refrigerate for 15 minutes.

For the glaze, melt the chocolate and butter together either in a double boiler or in the microwave.

Place the cooled brownie block on a wire rack with wax paper underneath the rack to catch the drips. Pour the chocolate overtop and let stand until it hardens. Once set, cut the block into squares or diamonds. It is easiest to cut neat squares when the brownie block is frozen.

Chef's tip | NEVER ICE BAKED GOODS WHEN WARM BECAUSE THE ICING WILL MELT AND WILL NOT ADHERE TO THE SURFACE.

BASE
2 squares (2 ounces / 50 g) bitter or unsweetened chocolate, chopped

¼ cup (60 mL) unsalted butter or margarine

1 cup (250 mL) sugar

2 large eggs, beaten

¼ teaspoon (1 mL) peppermint extract

½ cup (125 mL) all-purpose flour

pinch salt

FILLING
2 tablespoons (30 mL) unsalted butter or margarine, at room temperature

1 cup (250 mL) confectioners' sugar, sifted

1 tablespoon (15 mL) cream, milk or soy milk

GLAZE
3 squares (3 ounces / 75 g) semisweet chocolate

3 tablespoons (45 mL) unsalted butter or margarine

Italian Shortbread
with Almonds and Jam

MAKES: 16 BARS

A festive linzer-like square that is dainty and will add shimmering colour to any sweet table.

¾ cup (185 mL) unsalted butter or margarine, at room temperature

½ cup (125 mL) sugar

¼ teaspoon (1 mL) almond or vanilla extract

1 teaspoon (5 mL) freshly grated lemon zest

1½ cups (375 mL) unbleached all-purpose flour

½ teaspoon (2 mL) salt

½ cup (125 mL) apricot jam or any choice of jam

⅓ cup (75 mL) sliced almonds

Preheat oven to 350°F (180°C).

In a stand mixer, beat the butter and sugar for 3–4 minutes. Add the almond or vanilla extract and lemon zest and beat for 30 seconds.

In a small bowl, mix the flour and salt. Add to the butter and sugar mixture and beat until the dough is blended. The dough will be stiff.

Remove ½ cup (125 mL) of the dough and pat it down on a small plate in a thin layer. Place in the freezer for 15 minutes to harden.

Press the remaining dough evenly into either a 9-inch (23-cm) fluted springform pan or pie plate, or a 9 x 9-inch (2.5-L) pan. Spread the jam evenly over the dough to within an inch (2.5 cm) of the edge. Remove the remaining dough from the freezer and crumble it over the jam, allowing some jam to show through. You are creating a streusel effect.

Sprinkle with the almonds and bake for 30–35 minutes. Cool on a rack and cut into bars.

Cran-Caramel Streusel Squares

F D

MAKES: 24 SQUARES

A rich creation dripping with caramel and packed with cranberries and a crunchy streusel topping. An irresistible make-ahead treat.

Preheat oven to 350°F (180°C).

Lightly grease a 9 x 13-inch (3.5-L) baking dish.

Place the flour and confectioners' sugar in a food processor. Pulse until blended. Add the cold butter cubes. Pulse until the mixture begins to clump together. Turn out into the prepared baking dish. Press the dough firmly over the bottom of the pan. Bake for 20–25 minutes until the edges are golden brown. Remove from the oven and cool on a rack.

For the streusel topping, stir flour with the oats, both sugars and baking soda. Add the melted butter and stir until the mixture is crumbly. Set aside.

For the filling, stir the caramel sauce or butterscotch syrup with the flour. Stir in the cranberries, dates and pecans, if using, and spread over the warm baked base.

Sprinkle with the streusel mixture. Return the squares to the 350°F (180°C) oven. Bake for 35–40 minutes until the top is light brown. Remove from oven. Cool on a rack for at least 30 minutes. Cut into 24 squares, then cool completely in the baking dish. Store in an airtight container in the refrigerator for up to 1 week.

Freezing: These squares can be frozen wrapped tightly in foil for up to 3 months.

BASE
1½ cups (375 mL) all-purpose flour

½ cup (125 mL) confectioners' sugar

⅔ cup (150 mL) cold unsalted butter or margarine, cubed

STREUSEL TOPPING
½ cup (125 mL) all-purpose flour

½ cup (125 mL) rolled oats

2 tablespoons (30 mL) packed brown sugar

2 tablespoons (30 mL) sugar

¼ teaspoon (1 mL) baking soda

¼ cup (60 mL) unsalted butter or margarine, melted

FILLING
1 10-ounce (284-mL) can caramel sauce or butterscotch syrup

⅓ cup (75 mL) all-purpose flour

1 cup (250 mL) whole cranberries, fresh or frozen

1 10-ounce (300-g) container chopped pitted dates

1 cup (250 mL) coarsely chopped pecan pieces, optional

Chocolate Chunk Oatmeal Cookies

A classic favourite that appeals to everyone. To guarantee a blockbuster cookie, use high-quality chocolate.

½ cup (125 mL) unsalted butter or margarine, at room temperature

½ cup (125 mL) packed dark brown sugar

½ cup (125 mL) sugar

1 teaspoon (5 mL) vanilla extract

1 large egg

¾ cup (185 mL) all-purpose flour

½ teaspoon (2 mL) baking powder

1 cup (250 mL) rolled oats

1 cup (250 mL) chopped bittersweet chocolate or semisweet chocolate chips

Mix together the butter or margarine, sugars and vanilla until fluffy. Add the egg and beat until well combined.

In a separate bowl, mix the flour with the baking powder. Gradually add the flour mixture to the butter mixture (a few tablespoons at a time). Add the rolled oats and mix well. Stir in the chocolate and refrigerate for about 4 hours.

Preheat oven to 350°F (180°C).

Line a baking sheet with parchment paper.

Roll the dough into balls about 2–3 tablespoons (30–45 mL) in size. Place on the baking sheet, 2 inches (5 cm) apart. Bake for 10–12 minutes. Remove from the oven and cool on a rack for 15 minutes.

Variations: Add ½ cup (125 mL) of nuts (for example, walnuts, pecans or peanuts) if desired.

Freezing: Roll the dough into balls and flash freeze for 1 hour. Transfer into resealable plastic bags and store frozen for up to 3 months. Bake as needed from frozen.

Chef's tip | TO FLASH FREEZE BAKED GOODS, SPREAD ITEMS IN A SINGLE LAYER ON A BAKING SHEET AND FREEZE UNTIL SOLID. TRANSFER TO RESEALABLE BAGS FOR EASY STORAGE.

Chocolate Hamantaschen

FP

MAKES: 48 HAMANTASCHEN

A different take on a traditional Purim favourite. Hamantaschen are triangular cookies, often filled with dried fruit or poppy seeds. This super-chocolatey dough is very versatile and is easy to work with.

For the filling, beat the almond paste with the sugar in the bowl of a stand mixer until combined. Add the egg, then the flour and mix until smooth. Set aside.

For the dough, cream the margarine or butter in the mixer at medium speed until softened. Add half the flour then the sugar, cocoa, eggs, baking powder and salt. Mix until combined, scraping down the sides of the bowl if necessary. Stir in the remaining flour.

Divide the dough in half, wrap in plastic wrap and refrigerate for 1 hour.

Preheat oven to 350°F (180°C).

To assemble, remove half the chocolate dough from the refrigerator. On a lightly floured surface, roll the dough out to ¼-inch (5-mm) thickness. Cut into desired rounds with a cookie cutter or a glass. Spoon 1–2 teaspoons (5–10 mL) of filling into the centre of each round. Re-roll any scraps and cut out more circles.

To form the hamantaschen, lift three edges of the circle toward the filling and pinch each edge tightly. Repeat with the other half of the dough.

Place hamantaschen 2 inches (5 cm) apart on an ungreased cookie sheet—these cookies spread while baking. Bake until the edges are firm. Cool on a rack.

Variations: Fill with raspberry jam or chocolate chips. ♦ Shape any extra dough into a log, wrap in wax paper and freeze. Slice into ½-inch (1-cm) slices and decorate with coloured sprinkles before baking from frozen for a fast and easy activity to do with children.

FILLING
½ pound (250 g) almond paste

¼ cup (60 mL) sugar

1 large egg, at room temperature

1 tablespoon (15 mL) all-purpose flour

DOUGH
1⅓ cups (325 mL) margarine or unsalted butter

2½ cups (625 mL) all-purpose flour

1 scant cup (250 mL) sugar

⅔ cup (150 mL) cocoa powder

2 large eggs

1 teaspoon (5 mL) baking powder

½ teaspoon (2 mL) salt

Chef's tip | ALWAYS SIFT COCOA POWDER BEFORE USING AND ADDING IT TO RECIPES BECAUSE IT TENDS TO DEVELOP LUMPS.

Passover Mandlebread

F P

MAKES: 3 DOZEN COOKIES

A twice-baked almond cookie that can be enjoyed all year round. Easily prepared in advance and frozen.

3 large eggs

¾ cup (185 mL) sugar

¾ cup (185 mL) vegetable oil

2 tablespoons (30 mL) potato starch

¾ cup (185 mL) slivered almonds

½ teaspoon (2 mL) salt

1 teaspoon (5 mL) cinnamon

¾ cup (185 mL) matzo cake meal

¼ cup (60 mL) matzo meal

1 cup (250 mL) chopped semisweet chocolate or semisweet chocolate chips

1–2 tablespoons (15–30 mL) cinnamon sugar (see Chef's tip)

In a large bowl, beat together the eggs, sugar and oil. Add the potato starch, almonds, salt, cinnamon, cake meal, matzo meal and chocolate and stir until combined. The batter will be thick. Cover loosely and refrigerate overnight.

Preheat oven to 350°F (180°C).

Line a baking sheet with parchment paper. Moisten hands with a drop of oil and shape the dough into 2 rectangular logs. Place on the baking pan 2 inches (5 cm) apart.

Bake logs for 25–30 minutes. Cool for 5 minutes on a rack. Lower oven temperature setting to 325°F (160°C). Slice logs into ½-inch (1-cm) cookies and lay them on their side. Sprinkle with cinnamon sugar.

Return to the oven for 20 minutes. Turn cookies over and leave in the oven overnight with the heat turned off so they will dry out.

Chef's tip | TO MAKE CINNAMON SUGAR, COMBINE 1 TEASPOON (5 mL) CINNAMON AND 3 TEASPOONS (15 mL) SUGAR.

Shortbread for Passover

F D

These melt in your mouth! Do not even think about substituting margarine in this recipe!

Cream the butter and the sugar. Add the egg and beat well. Add the cake meal, potato starch and salt and mix until the flour disappears. Do not overmix.

Divide the dough in two and shape each piece into a log on wax paper. Wrap the ends and refrigerate for a couple of hours until firm.

Preheat oven to 375°F (190°C).

Line a baking sheet with parchment paper.

Slice the logs into rounds ½ inch (1 cm) thick and place on the baking sheet. Sprinkle with chopped nuts, if using. Bake for 12–15 minutes. The cookies should not turn golden but should stay white.

Cool on racks.

1 cup (250 mL) unsalted butter, at room temperature

1 cup (250 mL) sugar

1 large egg, at room temperature

1½ cups (375 mL) matzo cake meal

2 tablespoons (30 mL) potato starch

pinch salt

3 tablespoons (45 mL) chopped nuts, optional

Macaroons

MAKES: 12 COOKIES

What would Passover be without these coconut treasures?

½ cup (125 mL) sugar

2 cups (500 mL) shredded sweetened coconut

2 large egg whites

1½ tablespoons (22 mL) vanilla extract

pinch salt

¼ cup (60 mL) semisweet chocolate chips, optional

Preheat oven to 325°F (160°C).

Line a baking sheet with parchment paper.

In the bowl of a stand mixer, place the sugar, coconut, egg whites, vanilla, salt and chocolate chips, if using. Mix on low speed for 30 seconds then on medium-high for 1 minute.

Form the dough into 12 equal balls and place on the baking sheet. Bake for 25–30 minutes or until golden brown. Remove from the cookie sheet and cool on racks.

Variation: This recipe can be prepared by hand.

glossary

bain marie | a large, shallow pan of warm water into which a container (pan, bowl, soufflé dish) is placed. The food may be cooked in this manner either in an oven or on top of a range. This technique is designed to cook delicate dishes such as custards, sauces and savoury mousses without breaking or curdling them. It can also be used to keep cooked foods warm.

béchamel sauce | this basic French white sauce is made by stirring milk into a butter-flour roux. The thickness of the sauce depends on the proportions of flour and butter to milk. The proportions for a thin sauce would be 1 tablespoon (15 mL) each of butter and flour per 1 cup (250 mL) of milk; a medium sauce would be 2 tablespoons (30 mL) each of butter and flour; a thick sauce, 3 tablespoons (45 mL) each.

cheesecloth | cheesecloth has a multitude of culinary uses including straining liquids, forming a packet for herbs and spices that can be dropped into a soup or stock pot and lining moulds. It comes in both fine and coarse weaves and is available in gourmet shops, supermarkets and the kitchen section of many department stores.

chiffonade | thin strips or shreds of vegetables (classically, basil, sorrel and lettuce), either lightly sautéed or used raw as a garnish.

coating (i.e., coating the back of a spoon) | when a liquid or sauce "coats" the back of a spoon it is thick enough to use. Dip spoon in liquid, turn the spoon over and run your fingertip from the top to bottom of the back of the spoon—if a clear track is left, the sauce is "coating" the back of the spoon. If the track on the spoon is not clear, continue cooking the sauce a few minutes longer and test in the same way again.

deglaze | after food (usually meat) has been sautéed and the food and excess fat removed from the pan, deglazing is done by heating a small amount of liquid in the pan and stirring to loosen browned bits of food on the bottom. The liquid most often used is wine or stock. The resultant mixture often becomes a base for a sauce to accompany the food cooked in the pan.

dredge | to lightly coat food to be fried, as with flour, cornmeal or bread crumbs. This coating helps brown the food. Chicken, for example, might be dredged with flour before frying.

emulsion | a mixture of one liquid with another with which it does not normally combine smoothly—oil and water being the classic example. Emulsifying is done by slowly (sometimes drop by drop) adding one ingredient to another while at the same time mixing rapidly. This disperses and suspends minute droplets of one liquid throughout the other. Emulsified mixtures are usually thick and satiny in texture.

flash frozen/freezing | place items to be frozen on a baking sheet in the freezer and freeze until solid. Once firm, items can be transferred to resealable bags for easy and space-saving storage in the freezer.

fronds (as fennel) | the feathery leaves of fennel, referred to as "greenery".

julienne | foods that have been cut into thin, matchstick strips. The food (such as a potato) is first cut into ⅛ inch (3 mm) thick slices. The slices are stacked, then cut into ⅛ inch (3 mm) thick strips. The strips may then be cut into whatever length is desired.

mango, pitting | to pit a mango, stand the fruit on its butt end, and, with a sharp knife, cut from top to bottom parallel to both sides of the flat central pit. Score the flesh of each piece crisscross fashion, cutting to but not through the skin. Partially turn each piece inside out so the skin domes upward, exposing the cubes of flesh.

nori | these paper-thin sheets of dried seaweed can range in colour from dark green to dark purple to black. They have a sweet ocean taste and are popular in Japanese cuisine. Nori is generally used for wrapping sushi and rice balls. Japanese markets and some supermarkets carry nori either in plastic packaging or canned. All nori is very rich in protein, vitamins, calcium, iron and other minerals.

parchment paper | a heavy, grease- and moisture-resistant paper with a number of culinary uses including lining baking pans, wrapping foods that are to be baked en papillote and making disposable pastry bags. Parchment paper is available in gourmet kitchenware stores and many supermarkets.

rasp | a metal tool used to create lacy shards of zest. A zester or grater can be used instead.

roux | a mixture of flour and fat that, after being slowly cooked over low heat, is used to thicken mixtures such as soups and sauces. There are three classic roux—white, blond and brown. The colour and flavour are determined by the length of time the mixture is cooked. Both white roux and blond roux are made with butter. The former is cooked just until it begins to turn beige and the latter until pale golden. Both are used to thicken cream and white sauces and light soups. The fuller-flavoured brown roux can be made with butter, drippings or beef fat. It is cooked to a deep golden brown and used for rich, dark soups and sauces.

scallion | commonly called green onions. Scallions are available year-round but are at their peak during spring and summer. Choose those with crisp, bright green tops and a firm white base. Store, wrapped in a plastic bag, in the vegetable crisper section of the refrigerator for up to five days.

shallot | shallots are formed more like garlic than onions, with a head composed of multiple cloves, each covered with a thin, papery skin. The skin colour can vary from pale brown to pale gray to rose, and the off-white flesh is usually barely tinged with green or purple. Store dry shallots in a cool, dry, well-ventilated place for up to a month. Freeze-dried and dehydrated forms are also available. Shallots are favoured for their mild onion flavour and can be used in the same manner as onions.

score | to make shallow cuts (usually in a diamond pattern) in the surface of certain foods, such as meat or fish. This is done as a decoration on some foods (breads and meats), as a means of assisting flavour absorption (as with marinated foods), to tenderize less tender cuts of meat and to allow excess fat to drain during cooking.

sesame oil | sesame oil comes in two basic types. One is light in colour and flavour and has a deliciously nutty nuance. It is excellent for everything from salad dressings to sautéing. The darker, Asian sesame oil, also called toasted sesame oil, has a much stronger flavour and fragrance and is used as a flavour accent for some Asian dishes. Sesame oil is high in polyunsaturated fats, ranking fourth behind safflower, soybean and corn oil.

silpat mat | a silicon and fibreglass liner with a nonstick surface that can be used instead of parchment paper.

soufflé | a light, airy mixture that usually begins with a thick egg yolk–based sauce or purée that is lightened by stiffly beaten egg whites. Soufflés may be savoury or sweet, hot or cold. Baked soufflés are much more fragile than those that are chilled or frozen because the hot air trapped in the soufflé begins to escape (causing the mixture to deflate) as soon as the dish is removed from the oven.

watercress | watercress has small, crisp, dark green leaves. Its pungent flavour is slightly bitter and has a peppery snap. Watercress is available year-round and is customarily sold in small bouquets. Choose crisp leaves with deep, vibrant colour. Refrigerate in a plastic bag (or stems-down in a glass of water covered with a plastic bag) for up to five days. Wash, shake and trim stalk ends and dry watercress just before using.

index

corporate gift sponsors

Accent Home Products

L'Amour Hosiery

Annie Young Cosmétiques

Athens Fillo Dough

Banker's Pen (1991)

Bensus International

Boutique Mortimer Snodgrass

Claridge

Donald Berman Enterprises

Dollarama

Finesse Chocolates

Groupe Deux Printing

Loulou

Marcelle Cosmetics

RGC Coffee

Seraçon Candles

Stokes

Sub-Zero/Wolf

Wings

photo credits

Pages 1, 3, 4, 20, 21, 23, 28, 29, 30, 33, 41, 45, 50, 52, 55, 56, 57, 59, 61, 64, 67, 68, 69, 71, 75, 83, 86, 88, 91, 97, 100, 101, 103, 106, 109, 121, 125, 127, 133, 136, 138, 141, 146, 149, 152, 154, 155, 158, 161, 162, 163, 172, 174, 175, 176, 181, 183, 188, 193, 194, 197, 200, 207, 209, 211, 213, 215, 217, 223: NICHOLAS AMBERG

Page 5: THE SIR MORTIMER B. DAVIS JEWISH GENERAL HOSPITAL, MEDICAL PHOTOGRAPHY DEPARTMENT

Page 7: THE SIR MORTIMER B. DAVIS JEWISH GENERAL HOSPITAL, MEDICAL PHOTOGRAPHY DEPARTMENT

Page 9: COURTESY OF THE AUXILIARY OF THE SIR MORTIMER B. DAVIS JEWISH GENERAL HOSPITAL ARCHIVES

Page 10: COURTESY OF ODON WAGNER GALLERY

Pages 26, 74, 81, 115, 170, 185: SHAWNA GOODMAN-SONE

Pages 47, 85, 119, 206, 212: JONATHAN ROSS GOODMAN

Pages 63, 72, 73, 76, 98, 110, 131, 144, 165, 168, 171, 179, 187, 205: FOOD IN DETAIL BY BRAND-X PICTURES

Page 95: MARCY CLAMAN

Panache

Montreal's *flair* for kosher cooking

THE AUXILIARY OF THE SIR MORTIMER B. DAVIS JEWISH GENERAL HOSPITAL

3755 chemin de la Côte Ste. Catherine, #A 018, Montréal, Québec H3T 1E2

Tel: 514-340-8216   Fax: 514-340-7568

Email: lkaplans@aux.jgh.mcgill.ca

Panachecookbook.com

Please send me:

Panache: Montreal's flair for kosher cooking

Suggested retail price: $42.00

Quantity_____ $_____

Postage & handling (within Canada):
$7.00 for 1 book plus $1.00 for each additional book $_____

Postage & handling (to the US):
$12.00 for 1 book plus $2.00 for each additional book $_____

GST (Canadian orders only) $_____

Total enclosed $_____

Ship to:

Name _____

Address _____

City _____ Province_____ Postal code _____

Telephone _____ Email _____

Payment by (please circle one):   Visa   Mastercard   check (payable to JGH Auxiliary)

Card number _____ Expiration date _____

Name of cardholder _____

100 percent of the proceeds from *Panache* are going to support the JGH Emergency Department.

❧ THANK YOU FOR YOUR ORDER ❧